A DEEPER BEAUTY

Paramananda

A DEEPER BEAUTY

Buddhist Reflections on Everyday Life

WINDHORSE PUBLICATIONS

Published by
Windhorse Publications
169 Mill Road
Cambridge
CB1 3AN
United Kingdom

info@windhorsepublications.com
www.windhorsepublications.com

© Paramananda 2001, reprinted 2012

Printed by Bell & Bain Ltd, Glasgow

Cover design: Vincent Stokes
Cover photo: Corbis
Illustrations by Lucy Fallon

British Library Cataloguing in Publication Data:
A catalogue record for this book is available
from the British Library
ISBN: 978 1 899579 44 0

The publishers wish to acknowledge with gratitude permission to quote poems and extracts from the following:

pp.1–2   reprinted from *Friends, You Drank Some Darkness: Three Swedish Poets: Martinson, Ekelöf, and Tranströmer*, chosen and translated by Robert Bly, Beacon Press, Boston 1975. Copyright 1975 Robert Bly. Used with his permission.

pp.5–6   'Keeping Quiet' from *Extravagaria*, by Pablo Neruda, translated by Alastair Reid. Translation copyright © 1974 by Alastair Reid. Also reprinted by permission of Carmen Balcells Agencia Literaria SA, © Pablo Neruda 1958 and Fundación Pablo Neruda.

pp.19–20, pp.72–4 p.99   from John Stevens (trans.), *One Robe, One Bowl, The Zen Poetry of Ryokan*, Weatherhill, New York/Tokyo 1977.

p.29   'Hands ' is reprinted from *Complete Poems 1904–1962*, by E. E. Cummings, edited by George J.Firmage, by permission of W. W. Norton & Company. Copyright © 1991 by the Trustees for the E. E. Cummings Trust and George James Firmage.

pp.54–5 from *The Hundred Thousand Songs of Milarepa*, Shambhala Publications Inc., published by arrangement with Carol Publishing Group Inc., Secaucus, NJ, © 1962 Oriental Studies Foundation. All rights reserved. Reprinted by permission of Citadel Press/Kensington Publishing Corp. www.kensingtonbooks.com.

pp.69–70, pp.79–81   Miroslav Holub, 'What the Heart is Like' translated by Ewald Osers, 'A Boy's Head' translated by Ian Milner, from *Poems Before and After: Collected English Translations* by Miroslav Holub, Bloodaxe Books, 1990.

p.83   from Robert A. F. Thurman (trans.), *The Holy Teaching of Vimalakirti: A Mahayana Scripture*, copyright © 1976 The Pennsylvania State University.

CONTENTS

About the Author viii

INTRODUCTION 1

one   KEEPING QUIET 5

two   HANDS 29

three   JOY 45

four   BARING THE SOUL 69

five   BEYOND BELIEF 87

six   WALKING 103

seven   UNFIXING OURSELVES 119

eight   THE FISH 133

nine   ROMANCING DEATH 155

Appendix 171

Notes and References 187

Further Reading 189

Index 191

About the Author

Paramananda was born John Wilson in North London in 1955. From an early age he was curious about Eastern ideas, but it was not until the age of 23, after the death of his father, that his interest in Buddhism was aroused. At this time, the focus of his life shifted from the world of politics, in which he had been active, to more spiritual concerns.

During his twenties Paramananda worked mostly as a psychiatric social worker. He has also been involved in various types of voluntary work, including the Samaritans, drug detox, and more recently in a hospice.

In 1983 he came into contact with the Friends of the Western Buddhist Order and two years later was ordained into the Order itself. Since then he has been teaching meditation and Buddhism full-time. He sees meditation and Buddhism as powerful tools for both individual and social change, and believes that service to the community is a vital aspect of spiritual practice. From 1993 to 2001 he lived in California where he was chairman of the San Francisco Buddhist Center. He now lives in North London where he continues with his teaching and writing.

INTRODUCTION

I have been walking a while
on the frozen Swedish fields
and I have seen no one.

In other parts of the world
people are born, live, and die
in a constant human crush.

To be visible all the time – to live
in a swarm of eyes –
surely that leaves its mark on the face.
Features overlaid with clay.

The low voices rise and fall
as they divide up
heaven, shadows, grains of sand.

I have to be by myself
ten minutes every morning,

ten minutes every night,
— and nothing to be done!

We all line up to ask each other for help.

Millions.

One.

'Solitude 2', Tomas Tranströmer (trans. Robert Bly)

Sitting in my London flat on a rainy summer's day, trying to figure out what to say in this introduction, I pull from the shelf one of my favourite anthologies of poetry. I open the book at random and find the above verses, which I cannot remember reading before. It seems as good a place as any at which to begin. I am particularly struck by the image of a man walking alone across frozen fields — and the ten minutes the poet takes every morning and every evening to be by himself. It reminds me of meditation, time taken to be more fully with oneself.

This book has developed out of nearly twenty years of attempting to convey to others the meaning I sometimes find in Buddhist practice, in particular in meditation. I say 'sometimes' because the truth is that I often lose the thread of that practice. 'Being' a Buddhist meditation teacher has not insulated me from the confusion and periodic despair of life. Despite what follows, I do not always manage to be mindful or even simply kind. I am in some sense a constant failure. Nevertheless, I do feel that over the years I have made some small progress and I have become at least a little clearer about what is important to me.

If this book has a central theme it is the need to be ourselves, the relationship between this need and living in the world with others, and how to come more fully into the experience of being ourselves in such a way that this strengthened sense of ourselves finds a positive relationship with others and with the world at large. This in lives that are increasingly so full of activity and information that it often feels as though we are being pulled away from ourselves, pulled further and further away from a sense of who we are. Finding ourselves adrift in our lives with no sense of purpose beyond getting through each day with as much pleasure and as little pain as possible.

Perhaps I should say from the outset that I do not supply any definitive answers to the ills of modern life. I hope that on the whole I avoid telling you what you should and should not do. I hope that I raise points and issues that are worth taking a little time to reflect upon. Most importantly I hope that you, the reader, will be in some small way encouraged in your life. Despite the awful mess that we so often seem to make, on both a personal and a global level, there is something extraordinary about being here at all, and I hope that, like me, you will feel you would like to make the most of the magic of your life.

I have occasionally used terms not often found in books written from a Buddhist perspective; for example, I refer to the 'soul' in several places. If you know even a little about Buddhism you will know that it strongly rejects the eternalism implied by such a term. However, I employ it because for me it has a richness of texture that no other English term seems to convey; it implies something that cannot be fully expressed in the language of science or logic. I use it, then, poetically in order to convey that we as human beings are more than the sum total of our biological and environmental conditioning. I use poetry for the same reason.

So while, with the help of my editor, I have attempted to be as clear as possible, the book is suggestive rather than prescriptive, in that I have attempted to capture the 'atmosphere' of what Buddhist practice means to me. In the appendix I have outlined the two meditation practices I refer to in the text, in case you are not familiar with them, although there is no substitute for learning from a teacher, and with others.

Within the Buddhist tradition there has always been a strong emphasis on individual experience, and it is in this spirit that the book should be read, by which I mean don't take my word but judge what I have to say in the light of your own experience; some of it might ring true while some of it might not. Either way, I hope it encourages you to look afresh at your own practice – whatever that may be. In his poem 'Saint Francis and the Sow', Galway Kinnell writes

> The bud
> stands for all things,
> even for those things that don't flower,
> for everything flowers, from within, of self-blessing;

Meditation is a form of self-blessing that leads us deeper into our own hearts, and in so doing reveals a deeper beauty in the world around us.

KEEPING QUIET

Now we will count to twelve
and we will all keep still.

For once on the face of the earth,
let's not speak in any language;
let's stop for one second,
and not move our arms so much.

It would be an exotic moment
without rush, without engines;
we would all be together
in a sudden strangeness.

Fishermen in the cold sea
would not harm whales
and the man gathering salt
would look at his hurt hands.

Those who prepare green wars,
wars with gas, wars with fire,
victories with no survivors,
would put on clean clothes
and walk about with their brothers
in the shade, doing nothing.

What I want should not be confused
with total inactivity.
Life is what it is about;
I want no truck with death.

If we were not so single-minded
about keeping our lives moving,
and for once could do nothing,
perhaps a huge silence
might interrupt this sadness
of never understanding ourselves
and of threatening ourselves with death.
Perhaps the earth can teach us
as when everything seems dead
and later proves to be alive.

Now I'll count up to twelve
and you keep quiet and I will go.

'Keeping Quiet', Pablo Neruda

Some years ago, one of the people who attended the Buddhist centre where I worked gave me this poem. She knew I often read out a poem before meditation and thought I might like this one by Neruda. It usually takes a couple of readings for me to get hold of the sense of a poem, but in this case my response was immediate. The woman who brought it to my attention is a Spanish speaker, so a little while later, at a class, I had the poem read out in both the original Spanish and in the English translation I have used here. In Spanish the sounds of the simple words are very beautiful, and even in translation the poem retains some of that beauty. The meditation that followed the reading of Neruda's poem seemed to me to be quieter and more concentrated than usual.

Neruda seems to me to capture a simple but profound truth about the human condition, suggesting that much of the alienation that seems to characterize modern life has its roots in frantic overactivity, and that such activity cuts us off from the essential experience of being alive, alive in a living world of beauty and suffering. We are increasingly lost in activity, lost to our friends, our families, and ourselves. We are more and more out of touch with the rhythms of life. The frantic pace of our lives means we have little time for reflection, and no time to be still and reconnect with the underlying meaning of our lives.

For me, the poem could not but bring to mind the practice of meditation, which at its simplest is the practice of keeping still – keeping still not so much in the physical sense of sitting still, although such stillness can very much help us, but more in the sense of stillness of mind. At one of the places where I go on retreat there is a small pond. This pond is in the magnificent setting of the Santa Cruz mountains. After meditation I would often walk down to the pond and just sit. Sometimes the pond would be as smooth as glass. When it was completely calm like this, a leaf falling from one of the overhanging trees would set up a reaction that rippled out over the whole surface. It seems to me that the mind and heart are also rather like this. When they are calm they are able to respond to, and be affected by, all that touches them. Yet they are often so turbulent that a falling leaf goes completely unnoticed.

Keeping Our Lives Together

We are often frightened to think about our lives. We are fearful in case we find we have lost a sense of their having any real meaning. We feel hopeless in the face of bigger issues. We have little sense of being able to affect the world. Below our activity is a feeling of chaos. It is all we can do to keep our lives together. We try to avoid asking if we are happy with our jobs, our relationships, or the way we live. To ask such questions is to invite more doubt and despair. We have stopped really thinking because it does no good. Anyway, we don't have the time to think beyond the day-to-day.

Even when we go on holiday, we are behind a video camera, looking at the world as something once removed from us. Indeed, our world now comes to us out of the ether, impulses caught in cathode ray tubes. We are told what the weather is like outside our own door. We travel alone inside steel cages, to jobs that may bring us no real satisfaction. We accept all this in the name of progress. We accept the manufacture of armaments. We choose not to see the relations between the high levels of consumption in the Western industrial world and the exploitation and destabilization of other parts of the world. We are only dimly aware of the price that others pay for our high standard of affluence. We are powerless in the most powerful nations on the earth. We live in a democracy but do not trust the people we elect. We are not interested in politics because we feel we have no real influence. This is a bleak view of our modern world, but for many of us it is not far from the truth. In the words of Neruda:

If we were not so single minded about keeping our lives
    moving,
And for once could do nothing,
perhaps a huge silence might interrupt this sadness of
    never understanding ourselves
And of threatening ourselves with death.

This is a powerful idea: that if we stopped the frantic activity of our lives we would realize that under that activity is a sadness and sense of despair, and that this despair is caused by not understanding ourselves. There is a possibility that through just 'keeping still' a new awareness could arise: an awareness of ourselves, of one another, and a deeper sense of our relationship to the world. Neruda's stillness is a quality of mind, a mind that has the spaciousness to feel and to learn what is to be learned from the world around us.

Confidence Within

Perhaps what seems dead, but is really still alive, is the human soul, or genuine human qualities that have their roots in a deeper intimacy with ourselves. If we have a real awareness of ourselves we can also have the confidence to act from what is best in us. It is this kind of awareness and confidence that Plato attributes to Socrates in *The Apology*. Socrates is on trial for his life before 500 men of Athens because of his relentless pursuit of the truth and his tenacity in exposing the superficiality of others. He refuses to plead for his life and goes to his death with a peaceful heart in the knowledge that he has lived his life in the service of the good and the true. It is in *The Apology* that Socrates delivers the famous passage:

Some one will say: Yes, Socrates, but cannot you hold your tongue? ...
Now I have great difficulty in making you understand my answer to

this. For if I tell you that to do as you say would be a disobedience to the God, and therefore that I cannot hold my tongue, you will not believe that I am serious; and if I say again that daily to discourse about virtue, and of those other things about which you hear me examining myself and others, is the greatest good of man, and that the unexamined life is not worth living, you are still less likely to believe me.

Stepping Out of the World of Power

Reading Neruda's poem also brought to mind one of the many stories in the life of the Buddha. These stories tell us much about the Buddha's teaching, for it is from them that we can gain an impression of the Buddha's personality. We realize that he lived in a particular historical time, that he had friends and was part of the community in which he taught. There is a sense in which Enlightenment is outside time. As the highest human quality it is independent of time and place. Nevertheless, it has to have a real human form through which to express itself. I very much enjoy the stories about the life of the Buddha, both for their wisdom and because one builds up a picture of the man himself, living and teaching all those years ago in ancient India. This particular story involves King Ajatasattu.

◆◆◆

KING AJATASATTU was the son of King Bimbisara, who was a friend and follower of the Buddha. Ajatasattu, hungry for power, had once asked his father to relinquish the kingdom of Magadha in his favour. The king had happily agreed to his son's request because he desired nothing more than to be able to live a simple life, but the old king was revered and respected, and people still sought his counsel. Ajatasattu was jealous of the people's love of his father, so he imprisoned him and allowed him to starve to death. After ruling Magadha for many years, Ajatasattu became increasingly disillusioned with the trappings of power. Having ruled with intrigue and fear, he was now isolated and feared. On one particularly beautiful night, when the moon was full, he became overwhelmed by the evil life he had lived. He felt an intense need to find peace and freedom. After consulting his ministers he learned that the Buddha was staying deep in a nearby forest along with many followers. He decided to seek out the Buddha in the hope that he could tell him how to find peace for his troubled mind.

Ajatasattu set off in great pomp, seated on the royal elephant and accompanied by his wives and many attendants. The path narrowed and the king was eventually forced to dismount and continue on foot. As the forest became thicker, he had to abandon his retinue. With a single companion as a guide, he went deeper into the forest. Soon the king felt fear creeping over him. He began to imagine figures lurking behind the trees – assassins with swords and knives hidden in the shadows. His troubled mind was filled with fright. He became convinced he was being led into a trap. The hairs on his body stood on end and every little noise caused him to tremble in terror. He turned to his guide, Jivaka – on whose land the Buddha was staying – and in a trembling voice accused Jivaka of leading him to his death in the dark forest where the only sound was the occasional squawk of a jungle bird. How was it, Ajatasattu demanded, that the Buddha was here with many hundreds of followers, but there was no sound to be heard? Jivaka did his best to reassure the terrified king, telling him they were almost at the clearing where the Buddha was to be found. Hesitantly, and trembling like a child in a nightmare, Ajatasattu was led on.

Then they came upon a clearing. They saw the Buddha seated in complete stillness and silence, surrounded by many disciples. The clearing was lit by torches, and the whole company was bathed in a golden light. Such was the sense of calm and peace that came from the assembly that the king's fear suddenly fell away from him. Ajatasattu stood still, taking in the sight before him and allowing himself to absorb the serenity that filled the cool night air. It seemed to him that the figures sitting silently together radiated a tangible and deep contentment. Ajatasattu knew in his depths that this was what he sought. He felt the futility of his life, dominated by a mad lust for power, and while he stood there he had an intuition of another way to live – the possibility of a life pervaded by serenity and kindness.

In time the Buddha finished his meditation and indicated that the king might approach. The demeanour of the Buddha was so peaceful and full of love that the king became troubled by his past deeds. The king's questions had already been answered by what he had witnessed, but he nevertheless confessed to the Buddha his past evil acts and questioned the Buddha on how to find the peace he was seeking. The Buddha accepted his confession with compassion and answered his questions, encouraging him to put aside his evil ways and to give his life over to the cultivation of tranquillity and the doing of good. Ajatasattu teetered on the brink of making a fresh start and renouncing his craving for power, but in the end he was unable to do so. Muttering feebly under his breath that he had important business to attend to at the palace, he took his leave of the Buddha. After he left, the Buddha, with sadness in his voice, told the assembly that although the king had been deeply affected, touched to the core of his heart by the peace he had felt, he had not been able to change his life, so strong were the habits of mind that he had brought into being through his past misdeeds.[1]

◆ ◆ ◆

In the end, the king is unable to step out of the world of power. His fear and greed are too strongly ingrained. This is a good example of what Buddhism means by *karma*, which is often misunderstood. Throughout his life King Ajatasattu had expressed his lust for power to such a degree, and in such an extreme manner, that although deeply touched by his encounter with the Buddha, his past actions had acquired a volitional force that he was unable to control. His actions, which sprang from his mind, a mind dominated by a ruthless desire for power, nourished the emotion that was their progenitor.

Tha Karma of Everyday Life
Buddhism describes unethical actions as *akushala*. This term is often translated as 'unskilful', while *kushala* means 'skilful'. When we do something in a skilful way we are left with a sense of satisfaction, a positive sense of ourselves. When we act unskilfully we are left with a sense of shame or guilt. These feelings need not be dramatic, all the small volitional actions of our everyday lives are like the dripping of water that will in time erode the rock. Karma should not be understood as a law in the sense of a mathematical or legal law. 'If I do

something bad, something bad will happen to me,' is to have a simplistic and fatalistic view of karma. But it is not some cosmic tit for tat. What we do affects our minds. It really is that simple. We cannot say that any one mental state causes a particular action because we are faced with an infinite regression; the mental state that gave rise to the action has itself been conditioned by a previous action. We can perhaps say that our mental states and our actions are actively involved with each other, they are interdependent and cannot exist alone.

The consequence of an action is often experienced simultaneously with the action itself. As the words of hate come out of our mouths we feel our mind becoming more vindictive. Over time we become increasingly emotionally patterned. In certain situations we tend to react in predictable ways. When we find ourselves in a traffic jam we get angry and tense. After we make love we are left feeling alone and dissatisfied. When we see our mother-in-law.... If we reflect a little on our lives we can see how we often lack the flexibility and inventiveness needed to go beyond patterns of action and feeling that are negative and habitual. Understanding karma does not require some deep penetration into some esoteric and abstract law. It requires us to reflect upon our actions, the mental states behind those actions, and the consequences those actions have upon both ourselves and others. In short, it requires us to take more notice of our lives, to keep still sometimes, to reflect a little, to allow ourselves time to feel, to have a sense of ourselves as active ethical agents in the world.

When we are out of touch with ourselves, insensitive to our deeper values and feelings, we tend to act in unskilful ways. When we act from negative and confused states of mind we both suffer and reinforce those states of mind. The consequences are both immediate, in that we feel bad about how we have acted, and longer term.

Perhaps the way we have acted shapes another's idea of us, or alienates someone we love. It is not that some divine retribution is going to happen at some unknown point in the future, but that all our actions that have an emotional force behind them are constantly conditioning the tone of our mind. What we are, in terms of the mental states that we experience, is continuously being created. The way we live our lives is creating us.

Karma means actions of body, speech, or mind that have an emotional volition behind them. Buddhism calls the results of our actions *karma vipaka*. That our actions have consequences is plain common sense. It would be foolish to think that we are not affected by our actions. For our actions to have consequences they do not need to be as dramatic as the King Ajatasattu's, like imprisoning our own father. They are just the everyday decisions that we make. If we lead a life that has no time for reflection, no time to relate in a humane way to others, no time to nurture our own spirit, we will find in time that our ability to reflect, to relate, to act creatively and compassionately, will diminish, and, in the end, shrivel up altogether. This is the karma of everyday life.

The death of my father occurred at about the same time as the death of the father of a good friend of mine. My parents had had, on the whole, a happy and loving marriage and my father died at the relatively young age of 52 leaving my mother in a state of intense grief. But after a year or so my mother recovered and since then has very much enjoyed her life. By contrast, my friend's parents were very unhappy in their marriage, which was characterized by constant ill temper and mutual recrimination. His mother never recovered from the death of her husband, was unable to make a life for herself, and died a few years later – having seemingly given up on life. Though I cannot be sure, it seemed to me that while my mother was able to grieve and then go on to make the most of her life, my friend's mother remained attached to the past in a way that made it impossible for her to move on. The years of strife and irritation did not end with the death of her husband, but continued to influence her.

Reflecting on my own life, it is those times when I have acted in an uncaring way towards others that remain most vivid. I hope I have learned something from these unskilful actions, but it is quite easy to see how they can accumulate to such an extent that they darken one's whole life. This is the stuff of tragedy – a constant theme in Western literature. There is no escape from our unskilful actions; though we might think we have escaped through forgetfulness, the gods remember. But the reverse is also true, kindness has its influence as well. All our intentional actions have an effect on our minds and on our future. This, too, is the karma of everyday life.

The Beginning of the Path

Perhaps the biggest single factor affecting the way we behave is not out-and-out evil, but that we simply do not take the time to reflect. We act in haste. Our lives are too full to allow us to consider the effects of our actions upon ourselves and others. We suffer from a form of forgetfulness brought about through the lack of spaciousness.

Modern life is fast forgetting the human need to be still. The best loved of American poets, Walt Whitman, expresses this in the famous opening lines of his poem 'Song of Myself':

> I celebrate myself, and sing myself,
> And what I assume you shall assume,
> For every atom belonging to me as good belongs to you.
> I loafe and invite my soul,

I lean and loafe at my ease observing a spear of summer
    grass.

Whitman's loafing is the same as Neruda's stillness. Neither is talking
about wasting time; they are talking about using time to celebrate life
and to feel life deep in the body. They are pointing out that no truly
human life can happen without some means of refreshing, and
reconnecting with, oneself, and with life itself. At the very core of a
creative life is a feeling of community with all life. It is not that our
lives should be without striving or hard work, but if this activity does
not come from a deep sense of oneself and from a kind of stillness
where the mind and the heart are in communion, our actions will be
without real worth. Rather than bringing us the happiness we desire,
they will result in confusion and anxiety for ourselves and for others.

The first stage on the path that leads through the deep forest to
where the Buddha is to be found, is learning to sit still, learning to
be with ourselves in a simple, direct way. When we sit with our body
relaxed and alert, we actively begin to create the conditions that allow
us to hear the song of ourselves. When we relearn stillness, we can
begin to understand that it can exist in all our actions – as birdsong
deepens the stillness of a quiet wood. The stillness of action has a
clarity and spaciousness that is usually hidden by the rush and anxiety
of our lives. The most important thing we can do is give ourselves the
chance to connect more fully with what we might call our soul; the
human longing hidden under the sadness of our lives.

Opening Up
The sorrow that our frantic activity hides is related to feelings of
isolation, alienation, and disconnectedness. The Buddha's teachings
on the interdependent nature of all things offer a realistic resolution

to this sadness. The sadness is not done away with, but made conscious and put into the service of awareness and compassion.

From a Buddhist perspective, we act unskilfully because we are ignorant of the true nature of reality. What this means is that we see ourselves as independent and separate from the world, which we experience as being outside ourselves. This alienation from the world means that we tend to relate to it in a narrow and selfish manner. We see it either as something that can gratify our desires, or as something that frustrates and even threatens us. We are greedy for what we feel will gratify us, and fearful or angry at whatever appears to frustrate our desires. In so far as we relate to the world in this kind of way our behaviour is dominated by craving or aversion. To some degree this kind of response to the world is hard wired and necessary for our survival. For example, faced with a perceived threat our biological conditioning will kick in – the so-called fight or flight mechanism that also appears in many animals.

We do not often find ourselves in such threatening situations these days. On a day-to-day basis we are confronted with choices that are not so much a matter of survival as of psychological comfort or discomfort. So our choices are often made in order to protect our very limited sense of ourselves. Rather than being pleased for another's good fortune we feel somehow diminished by it, finding ourselves reacting in a resentful and jealous manner. Rather than opening up to others we are closed and defensive. The world is still perceived as fundamentally hostile to us. Of course, living is a dangerous affair, but to see the world in this way separates us from the world of which we are, by our very nature, a part.

It is one of the great tragedies of modern life that there is so much fear, even when we are perhaps more protected from danger than ever before. There seems to be an inverse relationship between security and openness. Years ago I heard a travel writer talking about her experiences of nomadic people. She pointed out that they were very open and generous and that it seemed that the more security people had, the more they felt suspicious of and threatened by others. The nomads had very little but were happy to share it. It was as though they did not regard anything as theirs but as common to all. Perhaps such an attitude stems from a deep connection to the natural world, where it is apparent that everything derives from the bounty of nature and cannot in reality be owned. Today we seem to have become obsessed with personal ownership, but rather than leading to a sense of security it makes us forever fearful of loss.

It has been well understood in many religious traditions that the search for material security is often psychologically and spiritually damaging. In the time of the Buddha, the spiritual aspirant would, if possible, being free from family responsibilities, give up everything except the bare necessities. This so-called 'going forth' from the worldly life was not seen as a form of self-imposed hardship but as stepping into a life of real freedom, a liberation from the cares and anxieties of the household life.

We do not have to give up everything in order to make progress in a spiritual sense, but there is a real need to understand that what we seek cannot be bought, and that the more we try to insulate ourselves from unhappiness through materialism, the more we find ourselves cut off from the sources of happiness, where 'everything seems dead' — cut off from others and ourselves.

Once again, many greedy people appear
No different from silkworms wrapped in cocoons.
Wealth and riches are all they love,
Never giving their minds or bodies a moment's rest.

Every year their natures deteriorate
While their vanity increases.
One morning death comes before
They can use even half their money.
Others happily receive their estate,
And the deceased's name is soon lost in darkness.
For such people there can only be great pity.[2]

Ryokan (trans. John Stevens)

In the Buddhist scriptures we sometimes find that those who spend their time pursuing money are regarded as lazy, in that they spend their time and effort on something that has no real worth. In both East and West there are of course many examples of individuals who have put their wealth to good use, but it is more common to find that the myth of King Midas is re-enacted, the accumulation of wealth leading to a psychological state of isolation. Greed is symbolic of a loss of human values, a mental state in which we have lost a feeling of belonging and connection with others, that sense of community with life. Perhaps at its root it is a feeling of unacknowledged fear; we seek an escape from death through the accumulation of material wealth. Something of this sort seems to underpin the modern work ethic, which has been traced back to the Reformation, when it became popular to believe that worldly success was a sign of having been chosen by God as one of the preordained, the 'logic' being that God would hardly allow worldly riches to be gained by someone he intended to cast into hell. Even today, poverty is often associated with a sense of moral failure.

It is, however, all too easy to dismiss all this as a cliché, to think that while materialism has often been warned against as leading to greed and hatred, this warning does not apply to us, that somehow we are immune.

It is all too easy for us to take on materialistic values in an unreflective way when we are so busy 'keeping our lives moving', easy to find ourselves driven by greed, to find that we have lost touch with ourselves, lost touch with the longing of our hearts to be in real relationship with others and with the world. What seems to be common to many individuals who can be broadly termed mystics is a deep appreciation of the natural world. It is an appreciation that is born from a type of 'being' in the world that is characterized by a balance between the receptive and the creative. This is often spoken of in terms of surrender, not in the sense of defeat but the victory of the heart over the narrowness of self-interest that keeps us isolated and alone. There is a movement from seeing the world as hostile – needing to be controlled and dominated – to a sense of belonging in the world.

In the San Francisco Museum of Modern Art is a large painting of a human heart held in a G-clamp. It is an arresting image. Standing before it I became more aware of a tightness in my chest and a desire to be more fully in relationship with both myself and the world at large, a desire to unclamp the heart. We cannot simply reach inside ourselves and remove the clamp. For most of us it has been tightened slowly over many years, and it will take time and effort to release it. It is all too tempting to believe that some intense cathartic experience will do it, but for most of us the release is a slow and sometimes painful experience, albeit punctuated by occasional moments of 'spiritual' intensity. The hard work has to be done in the everyday experiences of our daily lives: remembering to notice the trees, their autumn colours, finding a few encouraging and kindly words, noticing those times when we feel a tendency to pull back from others – and take a deep breath and step into intimacy rather than isolation, being less determined to impose ourselves on the world and more receptive to it, finding the courage to be still and feel the sorrow in our hearts so that real joy has a chance to manifest.

Perhaps the first step we can take towards reconnecting with our longing to feel part of the human community is simply to loaf a little. Take time to enjoy the natural world. Take ten minutes every morning and every evening to be alone.

reflection: Keeping Still

When you find yourself outdoors with a few minutes to spare, just stop, sit down or stand still – perhaps at a bus stop if you feel self-conscious about it – and come back to your breath. Relax your shoulders, soften your face, and just *be* for a while, free of the sense of having to do anything or get anywhere. Just breathe. Feel the ground under your feet, the air on your face. Let go of your interpretations and see if you can have a sense of just letting the world around you be as it is.

Imagine your senses are receptive to all that is around you, as if they are just open to the world without your having to make any effort.

Open your ears to all the sounds, letting whatever sounds there are come and go in your awareness. Don't listen. Just let the noises come to you. Try (but not too hard) to hear all the sounds without having to comment on them.

Now turn to what you see. Let objects just come and go, with no sense of searching them out or of resisting, or trying to hold on to them.

Soften to the world around you. Notice all the movement. Let yourself become a still calm point in all this movement. Try to become aware of the world in a receptive way, letting go of any feeling that it should somehow be different from how it actually is.

When thoughts about what is around you arise, see if you can treat them in the same way. Just let them be. Let them arise and fall away without adding more thoughts to them. Notice your tendency to comment on everything, and let it go. Imagine your mind as a mirror reflecting everything without discrimination. You don't have to comment on anything, naming it as good or bad. Simply be aware of whatever is happening around you. Just let it happen and witness it. Remember to breathe, and let the mind relax, letting go into your direct experience of the world.

As well as being aware of the external world, bring in any feelings or emotions that arise. Again, just let them come and go. Have a sense of the dynamic relationship between the external and internal worlds. Treat them as if they were just two aspects of the one reality. Let yourself feel part of the world around you.

reflection: Pausing for Thought

Get a sheet of paper and write at the top 'what people will say at my funeral'. Now without thinking about it just write whatever comes into your mind. To help you do this, keep the pen moving all the time until you get to the end of the page. If you can't 'think' what to say, write the last word again and again until a new one comes to mind – most importantly write quickly and without stopping until you have filled the page. Now read what you have written.

Try the exercise again using a different title such as 'what is important in my life', 'what has meaning for me', or 'what motivates me'. You can use these quick writing exercises to help gain a deeper sense of purpose and reveal your underlying volitions. Remember this only works if you keep your pen moving.

reflection: Letting Go of Things

Sit quietly in an upright posture, either on a cushion on the floor or in a chair. If you are sitting in a chair have your feet flat on the floor. Close your eyes, take a few slightly deeper breaths and allow the body to relax, without slumping, as you breathe out. Gently close your eyes, soften your face, and relax your brow and the small muscles around your eyes. Check that you are not holding your jaw. Let go of any tension in the shoulders. Imagine them falling back and down.

Just sit for a short while being aware of your breath, noticing how it feels as it enters and leaves your body. Let the breath move easily in and out of the body. Notice the discomfort if you try to control it, so just let it come and go in its natural rhythm.

Bring to mind the importance of your breath, knowing that although it is your most precious possession it cannot be held on to. Perhaps you can have a sense of your breath having been with you throughout your life, coming and going since the moment of your birth. Be aware that one day the breath will leave you and not return.

Now think of the things you own, and reflect that everything you think of as yours will one day be left behind. Imagine what you would like to happen to those things – your books, clothes, your house – when you die. Who would you like them to go to? Imagine giving them away to friends and family. Try not to get caught up in the practical details but focus on what it feels like to let go. If things get too complicated come back to an awareness of your breath, particularly the sensations in the chest.

Now think of one particular object you own, something you are attached to but no longer need. Try to imagine someone you know who would find joy in having this particular thing. Imagine yourself giving it away to them. How does it feel? Be aware of any feelings you have, perhaps conflicting ones. Don't try to make yourself feel how you think you should feel; just be aware of what emotions and thoughts are there. After a while, just come back to your breath once more. Sit for a while with your breath. Feel it coming and going in your body.

You will find the exercises in this book more useful if you take a few minutes to reflect on your experience afterwards. You might like to make a note of how you felt. With this particular exercise you might find you want to carry through what you have done in your imagination, that is, give something away to that person. If so, it might be a good idea to wait a couple of days to make sure you still feel the same.

two

HANDS

now all the fingers of this tree(darling)have
hands,and all the hands have people;and
more each particular person is(my love)
alive than every world can understand

and now you are and i am now and we're
a mystery which will never happen again,
a miracle which has never happened before—
and shining this our now must come to then

our then shall be some darkness during which
fingers are without hands;and i have no
you:and all trees are(any more than each
leafless)its silent in forevering snow

—but never fear(my own,my beautiful
my blossoming)for also then's until

 'Hands', E.E. Cummings

The human hand is incredibly sensitive. Packed with nerve endings, the hands are perhaps the easiest part of the body of which to be aware, and they can play an important role in meditation. We have learned to be aware of our hands almost without thinking, and strengthened the relationship between the mind and hands. Our hands seem to have an intelligence of their own because they are aware and full of mind.

Our hands allow us to interact with the world, express ourselves, communicate tenderness, give reassurance. The hands are full of character, and formed by the work they do. Some believe our future can be read in them. They are the most public part of the body, offered in greeting to strangers, and the means by which we express our most tender and intimate feelings.

We associate healing with the hands – as in the ancient tradition of the laying on of hands. We speak of people having green fingers, of being in safe hands. Hands feature in many sayings and metaphors. For the deaf, hands can be taught to speak, having a language of their own. They allow us to manipulate the world in countless ways. The severing of a hand was once regarded as a fitting punishment for theft, and there are a surprising number of folk stories in which the protagonist loses their hands. The hands seem to represent our being in the world, our ability to relate to life. The loss of the hands symbolizes the consequence of selfish actions that cut us off from the world in which we must learn to live co-operatively. It is with the hands that humankind has fashioned the world, and it is through the hands that the arts are born. When we first attempt complicated activities with our hands, such as playing the piano or typing, we say we are all fingers and thumbs, but once we have mastered the task it is as though the hands themselves have learned.

Discovering Our Hands

Oliver Sacks gives an account of a sixty-year-old woman, congenitally blind, with cerebral palsy. Clearly intelligent, the woman could not use her hands, which she described as 'useless godforsaken lumps of dough. They don't even feel part of me.' Sacks discovered that her hands, although seemingly useless, were physiologically normal. Because of her disabilities she never learned to use her hands. Everything had been done for her. Slowly, with help, the woman discovered the use of her hands, and they were restored to normal functioning. Indeed, they turned out to be full of sensitivity and beauty. The woman went on to become an accomplished sculptor.

To use our hands is to come into direct contact with the world. Sight and hearing imply a distance between us and the world. Touch means that the distance between us has been bridged. Subject and object are brought together. We are much more sensitive to what we touch than what we see. Only taste is a more intimate sense. But while it is quite possible to imagine living a life without taste, we cannot imagine a life without touch. While the whole body is tactile to a degree, it is left largely to the hands to be an active, searching expression of this sense. Those born without hands train their feet to perform as hands – so vital are they to us.

While awareness of our body is often quite diffuse, in the hands it can be precise. While we might be able to have only a general sense of our leg, for example, we can have a relatively strong sense of the hands. It is quite easy to imagine the delicate bones that form the hands, to sense the muscles and tendons. The hands are particularly sensitive to temperature, and full of sensation. The vitality of our bodies – our life force – can be felt in the hands. It is through our hands that we are in touch with the world, they become a portal into our own bodies.

Within the Zen tradition the hands are held in a very particular way during meditation; they are held in the 'cosmic mudra'. A *mudra* is a hand gesture with a symbolic significance. In the cosmic mudra the left hand is placed on top of the right, the joints of the middle fingers together. The thumbs are held lightly together, forming an oval. During meditation the hands are held against the body, level with the navel. It is as if you are holding the universe lightly in your hands. In this position the hands can be seen as an indicator of our mental state. They are like the flexible tip of a fishing rod acting as an amplifier of movement. If the mind drifts, the thumbs will tend to drift apart. If you become tense, the thumbs will start to press together. The hands, then, embody our mental states in a direct and assessable manner. So the hands act as a focal point. Keeping the hands soft and alert helps us to maintain our awareness.

It is not that the hands have a purely passive role; they are actively affecting as well as being affected. In the hands we can have a direct experience of what it means to use the body in meditation. While we might not find it comfortable to hold our hands in the cosmic mudra, we can still use the hands as a place to come back to during meditation. If we feel we are losing contact with the body, which is the foundation of meditation, a good way to re-establish our aware-ness is to bring the mind back to the hands. We can also strengthen our relationship with our hands outside of meditation. Whether we are working on a keyboard or doing chores, eating or preparing food, most of the time we are in some way or other using our hands – even when we are talking. Consciously paying more attention to the hands in a calm and relaxed way brings a new expansive dimension into our activity.

When the hands are fully alive – full of awareness – we gain a sense of the body's vital force, or what is variously known as *chi*, *ki*, or *prana*. In the East, rather than calling a person cowardly or brave, they will say his *chi* is weak or strong. An individual is understood to be deeply affected by their basic life force. Spiritual practice is often understood as working not so much on the psychological level, which so dominates the Western mind, but on a deeper level that transcends the duality of mind and body. We can have a direct experience of this non-duality in our hands, which, as the term 'cosmic mudra' suggests, can encourage a sense of interconnectedness with all life.

Although as we grow up, other senses – especially sight – become dominant, it is the sense of touch that first connects us to the world: being held and comforted in a parent's arms, and it is still through touch that we make our most intimate contact with others. According to the Bible, when Jesus rose from the dead one of the Apostles would not believe in the resurrection until they had touched his body. It is through touch that we reassure ourselves, and others, that the world is in place. If we trust our own eyes, we trust our sense of touch even more. Touch brings us into direct contact with the object and reassures us that it exists in the same manner that we exist. In the Metta Bhavana meditation (see Appendix) we learn to get in touch with ourselves, and be in touch with others.

If you are practising the Metta Bhavana, you can bring your attention to your hands. Feel the warmth and aliveness of the hands, or remember the tenderness that you have expressed through them. How does a hand full of kindness feel? What do our hands feel like when we think of an enemy?

A Deeper Beauty

When we take up meditation we open up the possibility of entering into a new relationship with our bodies. We often have a preoccupation with what we look like, a sense of ourself based on a superficial idea of visual beauty, conditioned by our culture. However, there is another, deeper, beauty that can come out of feeling at ease in our bodies and inhabiting our bodies fully. It is very striking that after a few days on retreat people begin to look quite different. Their faces relax, they begin to shine. The way they carry themselves changes. One of the things that can happen with a regular meditation practice is that we encourage an appreciation of the body as a vehicle for expressing ourselves in the world – rather than as an object to be viewed by others. If our sense of worth is based on having a perfect body, it will of course break down at some point. While it is good to look after ourselves, to over-invest in the body will at some point cause frustration and pain.

From a Buddhist point of view the body is important because it can be used to express values that matter to us. It is through the body that we can manifest kindness and awareness, so when we meditate we are concerned with gently encouraging an attitude of appreciation and kindness towards our bodies – with whatever limitations they might have, now or in the future. Personally, I have suffered from very poor eyesight since an early age. It has meant that I am unable to drive, almost a crime in modern America. It has restricted my life in many ways, and I am sure it has had a strong effect on my personality. However, this effect is quite mixed, and by no means all negative. It meant I became interested in more contemplative aspects of life, which have been a great source of joy. Of course, I would rather have better eyesight, and not have to worry that at some point it will fail altogether, but I am interested in working with the real situation – not wishing for what cannot be.

Most people have some difficulties with their bodies. Sometimes these can be put right, at other times they have to be accepted and we need to work within our limitations. Some years ago I heard that the most popular graduation present for girls in the USA was no longer a car but cosmetic breast surgery. It is a bizarre world where perfectly normal people feel they need to spend money on cosmetic surgery, while a third of the people in that most affluent country do not have access to reliable healthcare. Obsession with our physical selves leads to unhappiness and seeing others in a limited way. We often feel jealous and envious of others and, in the end, the mirror on the wall will show us this painful truth.

Social ideals of beauty are commercially and often cynically manipulated. When (or where) food was scarce, we find the ideal was often what we would now call obese. Now, however, people spend money to stay thin. Ever-increasing numbers voluntarily put themselves under the knife for the sake, not of their health, but of their looks. One of the strangest experiences I ever had was riding a night bus in Las Vegas (although there is no night there). Under the harsh blue-white lights the people around me looked at first glance quite young, yet there was something amiss, as if they were not quite what they seemed.... Most of the people on the bus were retired. Their faces had an unnatural tautness, where age should have softened the skins etching in character and experience, there was this waxy smoothness. Their lives had been successful enough to allow them to purchase cosmetic surgery and to gamble.

Interestingly, we can still appreciate the beauty of a face full of character and life well lived – as testified to by the enduring appeal of photographs of elderly native Americans. I have seen many a room decorated with a photograph of the deeply lined face of some Indian chief or other, yet we are constantly encouraged to believe that age is an enemy. In the fairy tale, *Snow White*, we are confronted with a mirror unable to lie, and in myth and literature – and throughout human history – vanity and cruelty are paired. Seeing our own bodies as objects on view robs the body of depth and richness that are the much needed virtues of old age.

Bliss-Bestowing Hands

The Buddhist tradition emphasizes both the limitations of the physical body and its preciousness. At first sight this might seem contradictory, but, as with so much of Buddhism, it is simply realistic. The limitations are clear: we grow old and we die. Along the way most of us suffer, to some degree or other, from ill health. It is common sense to do what we can to mitigate illness and try to make old age as comfortable as possible. But it is wilful stupidity to live in denial of the reality of our own old age and death. At some point such denial becomes a pitiable and humiliating state. The other side is that it is a wonderful thing to 'be' a human body. We might sometimes see a bird flying and think how incredible it would be to fly — to have that kind of freedom. But of course we also want the type of awareness that is able to appreciate and enjoy freedom.

Human awareness both creates and is created by our physical form. Buddhism teaches that consciousness precedes form. I am not sure I really understand what is meant by this teaching, but even if we take a modern evolutionary view, it is clear there is a dynamic relationship between what we can call the mind and the body, each affecting the other. In our hand we have a perfect example — the opposable thumb; there can be little doubt that our resulting physical dexterity has had an immense impact on our minds.

When I do a meditation on my body, I often find myself concentrating on the hands. I find them both physically fascinating and functionally wondrous. I often just bring to mind the different things I have done with my hands that day. I try to encourage an appreciation for my hands, to make an emotional connection with them. Such a connection is established by paying close attention to our actual experience on the level of sensation. What we are doing is coming into full mindfulness of our hands, mindfulness that includes the different levels on which our awareness operates. We have the level of bodily sensation, the level of emotion, and the level of thought. In actual experience these different levels cannot be neatly distinguished. They inform and strengthen each other. So within the hands we can consciously cultivate an integration of awareness that will bring us into a stronger relationship with ourselves. The same holds true for the rest of the body, but it is useful, however, to give ourselves a focus.

The Zen tradition has a very beautiful expression. After a practitioner has undergone training and achieved a level of tranquillity, they return to the market-place with 'bliss-bestowing hands'. That is to say, they re-enter the world and dedicate themselves to the service of others. Here the hands are invoked as a symbol of connectedness, a reaching out to others. The importance of coming into full relationship with ourselves is that it is through being fully aware of ourselves that we begin to have a real sense of our relationship with others and with life in general. The imagination required to have a connection with life has to be grounded in the experience of being alive. This experience is to be found within our own bodies, not in some disembodied state, which we might mistakenly think of as meditation. When we take the trouble to be aware of ourselves on the level of sensation, we are giving our experience a solid foundation. We include the earth element. It is through this element that we can find a sense of confidence. When we think of the Buddha we think of a seated figure whose posture clearly implies a connection with his surroundings, a connection through his physical experience.

Touching the Earth

When the Buddha was on the verge of attaining Enlightenment, he was challenged by Mara (the Buddhist equivalent of the devil). His response was to tap the ground and bring forth the Earth Goddess, who partly emerged from the earth to bear witness to his right to occupy the seat of Enlightenment, the Diamond Throne. This throne is not in some celestial heaven but under a great tree by a river in rural India. The Buddha does not ascend to a higher realm to attain Enlightenment. The symbolism is clear. Whatever elevated experience the Buddha has is rooted in the real world, in a fundamental connection to the world. The gesture of the Buddha's extending his right hand so that the fingers touch the ground is known as the earth-touching mudra: the mudra associated with the attainment of Enlightenment. It is a mudra that implies a connectedness with the world, a mudra to which the earth responds. Without this connection to the real world our practice will lack genuine human warmth; it becomes a refined kind of hedonism, a form of spiritualized escapism.

Our connection to life begins with a feeling for our own bodies, the development of a sensitivity to the body on the basic level of sensation, and the investigation of the body with a calm, clear mind. When we learn to sit with a sense of confidence we find that our body is full of surprises. Sometimes we experience our body full of life and vitality, filled with a feeling of joy We start to understand that our emotions have a sense base. We find that the relationship between body and mind is not dualistic, but one of closest intimacy. We find that consciousness exists as energy in the body, that the body can be infused with this subtle energy. Even pain can become a support for awareness. When the mind is confident and calm we become able not to instinctively pull away from pain while meditating, but to investigate the sensations we normally label as pain. When we do this, we often find these sensations are not in themselves unpleasant. We find they are constantly changing. We realize that much of what we experience as pain is our emotional reaction to sensations.

I am not advocating a form of masochism here. Severe pain should not be endured, because it is an indication that we are injuring the body and we should change our posture. But anyone who meditates will at times find a leg going to sleep, or an ache in the back. If we are able to avoid reacting to these mild discomforts and bring awareness to those areas, we find that our concentration can be deepened and the pain will often leave. It is something of a revelation to experience clearly the way we construct a sense of pain from what is often just a mild discomfort.

If we can experience this on a physical level it becomes a lot easier to understand that we do the same kind of thing on an emotional level. Much of our anger and frustration is built around simple experiences that we over-produce into grand opera. But we do have a choice. We do not have to give such importance to someone's careless remark. We can just let it be. We don't have to construct emotional dramas around our own, or others', lapses in awareness or kindness. It often seems as though we are primed to see the worst in others, to find life frustrating. Human conflicts seem so often to be one misunderstanding after another, and we soon find ourselves separated from each other by a complexity of emotion that is very difficult to unravel. But if we are able to respond calmly and kindly, touching the earth of our experience in some way, we often find that this enables others to do the same. What could have been a conflict can be turned around into a meaningful and positive exchange.

I am not suggesting that one becomes a passive doormat. Such a stance towards life stems from repressed anger and leads to depression and resentment. A calm, clear mind means you are able to judge when small things are best let go, while still having the awareness and sensitivity to know when it is necessary and appropriate to express yourself. We often react negatively towards others or repress our reactions, only to find ourselves resentful later. If we are clear how we feel, perhaps checking back with how our bodies feel, it is a lot easier to ask in a friendly manner for clarification from others when we are not sure what is being said or implied. If we are genuinely able to want to understand the other person, and can question them without any hostility, many potentially difficult and painful situations can be defused.

We seem to have come quite a way from our hands – yet they can be a place to begin a movement towards this kinder and more aware life, for such a movement begins by developing a compassionate and open relationship toward ourselves, at the basic level of the body: its sensations and the emotional and mental constructions that stem from them. When we are able to have an experience of appreciation for our hands, to feel their warmth and life, to connect with the tenderness they can express, to bring calm strong awareness into the palms and the fingers, then we will find the true meaning of the cosmic mudra and really hold the world in our hands.

reflection: Hands I

In meditation, try getting in touch with the body and the breath, then slowly bring your attention to your hands. Hold your hands in a relaxed manner on your lap – or you might like to try the cosmic mudra described on page 32.

Imagine that the hands are breathing along with the rest of the body, the air being inhaled and exhaled through the palms and the backs of the hands.

Feel all the tiny sensations in the hands that are forever coming and going. Encourage a sense of vitality, allowing the hands to be both relaxed and full of life. Perhaps imagine the delicate bones of the fingers in each hand. Let the breath soak through the skin; feel it in the soft flesh of the palms. Bring a loving awareness into your hands.

reflection: Hands 2

Consider all the things you have done with your hands since you woke up today. Encourage a sense of appreciation for them, through remembering the simple tasks of daily life such as washing and getting dressed, that you perform using your hands. Bring the awareness into your hands as fully as you are able.

Just sit for five or ten minutes, wherever you are, with your hands as your focus. Let the hands be soft and alive. Feel their warmth, let them breathe, imagine them full of kindness.

reflection: A Deeper Beauty

If you are practising the Metta Bhavana, you can bring your attention to your hands. Feel the warmth and aliveness of the hands, or remember the tenderness that you have expressed through them. How does a hand full of kindness feel? What do our hands feel like when we think of an enemy? Through meditation we can, over a period of time, develop an increasingly positive sense of ourselves. For many people this means we need to let go of certain social conditioning, e.g. ideas about what we should look like, and cultivate a sense of appreciation for how we really are.

Try sitting in meditation posture, taking a little time to relax and calm the mind, then just bring to mind your five senses in turn.

For example, think about the sense of sight, all you have seen in your life, all that is still to be seen. How wonderful it is to look out at the ocean or look into the face of a loved one. Be aware that this ability to engage with the world on a visual level is a consequence of having a human body and reflexive awareness. Have a sense of the richness of the world that comes to you through your eyes. Have a sense of gratitude for your sense of sight.

Do the same with your other senses. Be aware of the world as full of smells and textures, sounds and tastes. A world that is rich because you are able to perceive it through the senses given you by your body and mind. Think about how your body allows you to move in the world. How your arms and hands allow you to interact with the world around you. Try to develop a awareness of your body in relation to how it allows you to be in the world, rather than based on how you think others might see it.

three

JOY

Over the years that I have practised Buddhism, I have noticed that although Buddhists tend to be noticeably more mindful than non-Buddhists, perhaps more helpful and considerate too, they have not struck me as more joyful. Some Buddhist centres even have a rather sombre atmosphere. I once took a Buddhist friend, who was over from England, to a large American Zen centre. After we had looked around, he commented that the place felt like a mausoleum, which seemed to me a fair assessment. Sangharakshita, my teacher, who spent many years in India, has remarked that much English Buddhism often seems a very worthy but rather sanctimonious affair (or words to that effect). Yet he found it quite different in India, where people seem to approach their practice of the Buddha's teachings with real joy, particularly at celebrations such as Buddha Day.

Some years ago I visited a Tibetan Buddhist centre in France. They had recently held a ritual for an important teacher who had died. This ritual was conducted by two Tibetan lamas, who seemed to be sharing a private joke, and some of the students were quite upset at this attitude, which they felt indicated a lack of respect for their departed teacher. While it is understandable that they were upset, this does seem to me to illustrate both a different attitude towards spiritual practice and, perhaps, more profoundly, towards life itself.

More recently, I visited a number of Chinese and Tibetan Buddhist monasteries. I was moved by the combination of devotion and cheerfulness the non-Western pilgrims displayed. In particular, many of the Tibetans seemed delighted to see a Westerner turning the prayer wheels or kneeling beside them at the shrines. While they spoke no English and I spoke no Tibetan, they would often stop me with beaming smiles and thumbs-up signs, and leave me in no doubt as to the happiness they felt in our shared devotion.

There does, by contrast, seem to be a lack of joy in Western Buddhism. This may be due partly to temperament and partly to inherited ideas of what religion is. There are of course exceptions to this, but I suspect these are naturally joyful people, and their quality of taking delight in the spiritual life has managed to withstand this more gloomy atmosphere. Perhaps in the West we have been conditioned to regard spiritual development as a serious and sombre affair?

Perhaps, also, people's approach to the Dharma is often dominated by a negation of themselves that stems from a superficial understanding of the idea of 'non-self', and such terms as 'overcoming the ego'. Buddhists often seem to be more concerned with what they shouldn't do than with what they should do (which of course very much includes the cultivation of a happy and joyful attitude towards the ups and downs of life). It seems that many Westerners understand the Buddhist precepts (ethical guidelines) primarily as prohibitions, rather than seeing them as opportunities for the positive expression of awareness and compassion. Western Buddhists often seem a little stiff, as if, in them, the valuable practice of mindfulness finds its emotional energy in the will, rather than from calmness and clarity. A clear, still pond ripples at the slightest breeze. A calm, clear mind is forever ready to respond to the world around it.

Mindfulness is not primarily a matter of restraint, although that is sometimes valuable. It is better understood in terms of a freshness and responsiveness to all aspects of our experience. I have sometimes wondered if a lot of meditation is good for Westerners if it is not balanced by a joyful expression of some sort. Meditation can help us to realize that we can, and need to, experience ourselves fully, in an unrestrained manner – without always expressing it outwardly. Realizing that we can make a choice about how we behave in the world based on a fuller awareness, rather than on repression, is of fundamental importance in maintaining joy in our lives. While it is important to avoid inflicting our negative emotions on others, it is just as important to give ourselves the freedom to fully express positive mental states.

Within meditation we have a chance to become more familiar with our emotional energies within a context that provides a sense of containment and clarity. We learn that the full range of our human emotions can be experienced without the necessity to act them out. Meditation allows us the leisure to experience the richness of the human heart – but it also teaches us that there is a choice – and a difference – between experience and expression.

Directing Our Minds

Related to this alienated kind of mindfulness, and lack of joy, there often seems to be an emphasis on meditation being a struggle, and on the eradication of the natural liveliness of the human mind. The aim of meditation is to direct the energy of the mind, not to control the mind by repressing its natural curiosity and spontaneity.

Meditation aims to encourage a state of awareness characterized by openness and flexibility, free from anxiety and fear.

Our approach to meditation should not be one of wanting to dominate the mind or of seeing ourselves locked in some epic struggle with an evil ego. Such an attitude is often based on a kind of inverted inflated view of ourselves. Self-flagellation is not part of the Buddhist tradition, which regards severe asceticism as just as misguided as unheedful hedonism.

Nor, when we experience difficulties in meditation, should we give up. This often happens if our practice is too idealistic. If we have an unrealistic notion of ourselves – Enlightenment or bust – the chances are we will bust. The false notions that we are likely to gain full Enlightenment some time next week, or that we are so bad that no amount of practice will ever do more than scratch the surface of our dark souls, are equally undermining in the long run. So when things get a little difficult we should try to lighten up a little and see things with a bit of humour.

Our minds are often like those of small children. We can try to deal with a situation through stern discipline or we can enter into a more playful and interested relationship with ourselves. Of course, completely free parenting does not work; we need a balanced approach. So while there is a real need for some degree of discipline if we are serious about meditation, to get ourselves to the cushion on a regular basis, we do not need to be too rigid. I have known some people who, when for some reason they have been unable to meditate at their usual time, become quite distressed. It is as if they regard their meditation as a daily fix and they will go into some awful DTs if they are unable to do it. Of course we have to be careful that we are not just being lazy and finding all these good reasons why we can't meditate today, but fretting about the rare occasion when it really is not possible seems to me a little neurotic.

It is hard to talk about what really goes on in meditation. We are using the mind to work with the mind. It is like massaging one hand with the other. It is very difficult to separate clearly the sensation of one hand from the other. The self-reflective part of our awareness is not clearly distinguished from the rest of our mind, of which it is aware. For any sort of meditation to happen there has to be some element of this self-reflective awareness. We have to be aware that we are aware. It is then very easy to see the mind as dualistic, one part of it trying to control the other. A good part, a 'grown-up' part that wants to be a 'good Buddhist' tries to control another part that is seen as, well, evil, or at least rather naughty. For most people it is rare to become sufficiently concentrated to experience the mind as an integrated whole. While it often feels as though there is a good mind versus a bad mind, this is not a very useful attitude to take.

So while we can talk about meditation as the mind working directly on the mind, we should try not to regard those aspects of our experience that are less under our conscious control as something requiring eradication. Through a patient, kindly approach we can gradually involve all our psychic energies in our meditation. Indeed, it is the engagement of the aspects of our mind that are not subject to our will that gives meditation its depth and richness. Meditation is a place where our wilful 'should-be-ness' can be relaxed. We move towards an experience of ourselves as a textured and complex individual, where the sometimes conflicting aspects of ourselves can at least get a sense of each other. If meditation is a mental training, it is a training based in love rather than force. It is a means by which we can begin to heal the internal conflicts that thrive in the black-and-white atmosphere of dualistic thought, the good mind versus the bad.

Big Mind

We each have only one mind, even though at times it doesn't feel like it. The good mind and the bad mind are one and the same, as expressed in the wonderfully prosaic term popularized in the West by Shunryu Suzuki, 'big mind'.[3] Big mind captures the experience of heightened awareness that can occur in meditation. It is not the self-reflective part of us watching over us like Big Brother, but our whole mind, saturated with awareness. Although our actual experience of what we can call big mind might be quite limited, we should nevertheless strive to bring such an understanding to our meditation. Although our mind often feels fragmented or divided against itself we should remember big mind, and remind ourselves that behind the confusion is at least the possibility of a sense of clarity and expansiveness where all our conflicting mental and emotional experiences disappear into a calm, pure awareness. We can perhaps think of a vast ocean that on the surface is whipped into mighty waves, but further down, in the depths, is calm.

Big mind is like big heart — it is open to what is actually there. It is patient and it is forgiving. It does not enter a situation with the idea of a fixed outcome. 'This situation will be like this' is not the attitude of big mind. The first thing is to take an interest in what is actually going on. If we go in with an idea of how things should be, and they are different, we get very frustrated. Perhaps our parents thought we would enjoy playing the piano, but we didn't — it was a fine day and we would have preferred to play with our friends. Even our parents hated the racket we resentfully made. If we want someone to learn we need to sit down and learn with them. To enjoy playing a piano a child needs the parent to be actively interested in what is happening, and the parent needs to be open to learning in order fully to take part. Similarly, if we pit one part of our mind against another in meditation, we will find it very hard to find real joy. There will always be some resistance to what we are doing.

Big mind takes in the whole situation. It enters into the situation completely. It is not one part of the mind trying to impose its will on another.

The most common way we split the mind is into intellect and emotion. We think we should do something, but we have no real emotional energy invested in it. Depending on our personality, we might do it anyway or we might just give up. One of the reasons we meditate is to try to bring these two facets of ourselves together and encourage a unification of heart and mind. Big mind is the ability to encompass the divisions that exist within ourselves and to seek a creative way of working with them.

It is sometimes necessary to do things even when we do not feel wholehearted about them. With meditation, too, there has to be some discipline. We may not always feel like doing it, but this does not mean that we cannot at least acknowledge the part of us that isn't very interested. We have to be able to pay attention to ourselves in this way, to see both sides of ourselves. When we do this a third element can arise that is not so dualistic, but more concerned with working with the whole of us. This part of us is what we meditate with. It is a self-awareness that is above, but also encompasses, the conflicting parts of ourselves. This kind of self-awareness can arise when there is some kind of dialogue between the divergent aspects of our mind. The 'good idea' part of us has to value the energy that is pulling in another direction.

This energy is often where our imagination is. It is only when we are able to engage this kind of energy that some real sense of vision can arise, and it is this sense of vision that sustains us in the spiritual life. There needs to be a sense of excitement and joy in our practice, a sense that what we are doing is of real worth. This also has to be nurtured outside meditation. We cannot expect it just to be there when we sit down to meditate, if the rest of the time we neglect it. This means that we need to stimulate the emotional side of ourselves, and in particular find ways of cultivating a sense of excitement about the spiritual life and, through reflection and reading, reminding ourselves of the benefits that meditation and ethics can bring.

Flexible Awareness

I have often been struck by the number of people who do not seem to enjoy their meditation, especially those who have an established practice. In some ways it is laudable that they keep trying. If you meditate regularly there are bound to be times when it is difficult, but in order to sustain a beneficial practice there needs to be a strong element of enjoyment at least some of the time. It is not enough that we think meditation is good for us and we therefore force ourselves to do it. Rather, the direct experience of meditation needs to be sustaining. Part of the problem is having a fixed idea of what should happen when we meditate, what our mind should be like.

It reminds me a little of the local gym, where many people appear to be at war with their bodies – no pain, no gain. They seem to want to force their bodies into an unnatural shape that conforms to some idea they have, but bears little relationship to their particular type of body. Why do people meditate if they do not enjoy it? Why do they continue to approach it in the same old way if it brings them little joy?

I recently led a workshop for quite experienced meditators. One woman, who had been meditating for seven years, had been taught the form of Mindfulness of Breathing in which one counts the breaths. She said she had never found this counting useful. Counting made her tense and anxious. I asked her why, after seven years, she was still counting her breaths. Her response was that this was how she had been taught. This situation highlights the need to get into dialogue with other meditators, especially those with more experience than ourselves, if at all possible. I suggested she tried it without the counting to see if it worked better, for although this approach seems effective for most people, perhaps it was not the best one for her. The main thing seemed to be that she needed to enjoy her breath rather than seeing the practice as a chore.

I was reminded of the story of the devoted peasant who was given a mantra by a passing guru, which he misheard so that the sacred syllable *hum* was replaced by a similar Tibetan word meaning 'cow'. The peasant chanted this mantra to good effect until the guru returned to the isolated village to check on his progress. On discovering the mistake he carefully corrected the pronunciation. However, the correct mantra seemed not to work, and the beneficial effects of the practice were lost. Some time later, on a third visit, the guru gave his pupil special permission to revert to his original version, and once again the peasant began to experience the benefit of his heartfelt invocation of the cow.

We need to trust our experience and feel free to try different approaches that might work better. There are forms of the Mindfulness of Breathing that do not employ counting. The initial delight we find in meditation is often lost because we become too rigid in our employment of technique. Our practice becomes a routine that we go through regardless of our experience, like going to the gym and feeling we have to do so many press-ups or swim a certain number of lengths.

The most important quality we try to encourage when we meditate is awareness. The various techniques are there to help us do this.

We need to keep in mind the nature of the awareness that we are trying to develop – not a rigid awareness that is insensitive to our real experience, but an open, flexible awareness that can respond to our actual situation.

A friend and I were once walking along a beach, and we were passed by a number of joggers. Most of them seemed to be in some state of distress. We then came upon a young woman exercising. I don't know if she was employing some system of exercise or just making it up as she went along, but what she was doing reminded me of the spontaneous joy of a young child. She was jumping and skipping, throwing her arms in the air. It was quite wonderful to watch. Her body seemed to be full of joy and life. She seemed open to the wind and the sea, and appeared to be really enjoying herself. At the same time her movements were graceful and co-ordinated, all in striking contrast to the desperate joggers. I thought, 'this is what the mind should be like when we are meditating.' It reminded me of Milarepa's 'Song of a Yogi's Joy'.

Milarepa was an eleventh-century Buddhist poet famous for the depth of his meditation and the expression of his profound experience in spontaneous song:

> The greater the distress and passions,
> The more one can be blithe and gay!
> What happiness to feel no ailment or illness;
> What happiness to feel that joy and suffering are one;
> What happiness to play in bodily movement
> With the power aroused by Yoga.
> To jump and to run, to dance and leap, is more joyful still.
>
> What happiness to sing the victorious song,
> What happiness to chant and hum,

More joyful still to talk and loudly sing!
Happy in the mind, powerful and confident,
Steeped in the realm of Totality.

Milarepa is clearly expressing a profound state in which dualism has been overcome. What comes through is a real sense of joy. We might be a long way from being able to respond to our distress in the same manner as Milarepa, but we can encourage an attitude of interest and joy. On the most basic level we need to frame our practice in a manner that allows us to take delight in it. We could think of ourselves as poor human beings lacking in awareness and compassion, desperately needing to meditate in a frantic attempt to improve a little. But such a view does not allow for the possibility of joy and delight in meditation; it limits us even before we take our seat. Conversely, we can encourage the idea that as humans we have a tremendous potential, that we can build on our existing awareness and nurture the kindness that we already experience.

The Joy of No Comparisons

The scriptures of Buddhism are full of accounts of the most unlikely characters gaining insight into Reality. Milarepa himself had a rather unpromising start. After the death of his father, his uncle, now the head of the family, plotted to steal the family's wealth and land. Milarepa's mother was reduced to a state of penury and treated little better than a slave in her own home. Under the influence of his embittered mother the young Milarepa learned the black arts and used them to take revenge not only on his uncle but on the whole village, who had stood by while his family had been cheated and humiliated. Later, having been responsible for the deaths of many people, Milarepa had to undergo many hardships before he attained the joyful state of liberation to which his songs testify.

Few of us start from such a position, weighed down by such a murderous past, but the extreme life of Milarepa illustrates the potential we all have to transcend the limitations of a life dominated by greed and hatred. Most of us in the West have a tremendous opportunity to cultivate ourselves. We are relatively free from the hardships faced by most of the world's people. We live in a society where we have the freedom to practise, and we have access to a great many resources to support our efforts. What we often seem to lack is a basic confidence in ourselves and a joyful relationship to life. Confidence, in the modern world, seems to be based mainly in a sense that we are in some way better than others. From an ever earlier age, children are encouraged to see themselves in a competitive relationship with one another, their sense of worth linked to the achievement of external goals.

In Buddhism, it is regarded as arrogant to think of ourselves as better than someone else. It is also said to be a form of arrogance to think of oneself as inferior to another, or even the same as another. Here, Buddhism is trying to help us to see that comparing ourselves to others is beside the point. It is not a useful way to view either ourselves or other people. It is quite ridiculous for a child to be conditioned to feel that self-worth depends on making the school basketball team, or being top of their class. Instead of children being encouraged to find joy in sport or literature, they are pitted against one another.

When we internalize this kind of attitude as a child it is very hard to let go of it later. We find it a particularly great handicap if we wish to develop as individuals. When we meditate we will have in the back of our minds the idea that we are either a better or a worse meditator than other people. This is, of course, a quite meaningless idea. Spiritual practice is not something we can measure and compare. We can find ourselves looking at the spiritual life as if it is some kind of competitive sport, constantly concerned with how we are doing in relation to others. Not only does this lead to anxiety, it also means that we cannot really encourage and support others, because we are jealous that they might outdo us. Rather than feeling joy in our own, and others', progress we are caught up in ideas of superiority and inferiority. Confidence does not arise by encouraging ourselves to feel better than others, but by valuing the progress made.

Meditating with other people can be a great support to our own practice. We feel supported in the sense that others affirm that what we are trying to do is of real worth. If we are a little sensitive to those around us we will find that we can tune in to someone else's concentration, and allow the general atmosphere of awareness to help us. We can have a tangible experience of being part of a great tradition that goes back to the historical Buddha, and includes many outstanding figures like Milarepa. We are working with the same basic stuff they had to work with – human awareness. The difficulties we might encounter have been encountered – and overcome – by many thousands before us. We then have to encourage a basic confidence in our own ability to cultivate awareness and compassion. This does not mean having some overblown idea of ourselves as one step away from being a Buddha, but a quiet appreciation of the progress we are making – and a sense that, although it takes time and effort, there is really no limit to our practice.

It is not that one day we will be done with spiritual practice. As we progress, it opens up rather than narrows down. If we have a rigid idea of wanting to reach the end we will find the spiritual life very frustrating. It is as if we are in a rush to get to the top of a hill: we climb what we think is the final ridge only to find that the hill goes on and on. So it is with our spiritual practice. We need to have a general sense of direction but at the same time take in and enjoy the landscape as we go.

I sometimes play with this idea when I teach walking meditation. I instruct people in a very slow form of walking in which we take one small step with each breath. People often find this quite hard because they feel they are getting nowhere. When I sense that people are getting frustrated, I tell them to imagine that this is all we will be doing tonight, just walking very slowly together, for the next two hours. If people can let go of the idea of there being some fixed destination, they are often able to relax into what is really happening. It is hard to express in words just how wonderful it can be to walk slowly with others, being aware of oneself and of one another. There is a simple joy in such an activity, a sense of connectedness and completeness – just from walking in a circle without hurry.

Whenever we begin to feel frustrated in what we are doing, we should slow down and pay closer attention to it. Frustration takes us away from ourselves; we become alienated from our experience. When we feel this beginning to happen we need to pay more attention to our experience. I used to live with someone who was a great cook, but he was very messy and seemed to use every pan in the house. After a meal the kitchen would be in a state of chaos. Because I was home in the morning, my writing time, I was often confronted with the chaos from the night before. I found it very interesting to become aware of my reaction as I set about cleaning up. I tried to just take the time it needed, not rushing to return to my writing, but trying to find some pleasure in cleaning up. If I found myself beginning to feel resentful I would remind myself what a nice meal I'd had the night before. I would slow down and try to enjoy the experience of restoring order. The point is that if I had rushed through it feeling resentful and put upon, by the time I got down to what I wanted to do, I would have created frustration and distraction. I would then find that I was not able to work effectively. Then of course I would get into an even worse state. Alternatively, I could see it as a useful way to become more aware of myself and actually supporting my next activity. I don't want to give you the impression I can always to do this, but I do manage it some of the time.

This, then, is a small example of what is going on all the time in our lives. It can go on in the sense of wishing to be done with a particular activity, but it can also go on in the overall context of our lives. In perhaps its most extreme form it can be a whole life wasted doing something in which we really have no passion or true interest. Sometimes this is called becoming 'a success'.

Changing Our Relationship to Time

It may at first seem a harsh statement, but Buddhism sometimes talks of most human lives as basically being wasted. It is as if we throw away what is most dear to us. From a Buddhist perspective human life is rare and precious. Having a human form is a unique and wonderful opportunity. While we take being human for granted, Buddhism calls on us to see it as an exceptional, almost miraculous, occurrence. Possessing a human form and a human consciousness makes possible the unlimited expression of love and awareness. What is more, and is in a sense profoundly ironic, is that we somehow intuitively know it is true. What else could explain human beings proving themselves, again and again, willing and capable of acting from love – even at the cost of their own lives? We sense our capacity to act for the good as surely as we fear our capacity to act from the bad. It sometimes seems to me that much of my life is lived as if I am caught in the headlights of my possible actions. I fear doing evil, but I lack the courage to do good. I can feel startled and paralysed. I see my meditation practice as attempting to bring a spaciousness and joy into my life. Then following the good can become a form of playfulness.

It seems wonderful to me that many of us, when faced with extreme conditions, behave with such courage and humanity. I have seen this in the way many face their own death or the death of those dear to them. But it also seems to me a great pity that we perhaps have to find ourselves in extreme and painful situations before we find the courage to tap into such goodness.

The remarkable autobiography of Jean-Dominique Bauby, *The Diving-Bell and the Butterfly*, recounts his experience of suffering a severe stroke which left him completely paralysed. Formerly a successful and urbane fashion editor, Bauby manages to dictate his memoir by a laborious semaphore of fluttering an eyelid – the only part of his body still capable of voluntary movement. What is revealed is that through the trauma and desolation of his condition, a new sense of being alive to the world has emerged. Bauby here recounts a trip from the hospital:

> *I have come to gorge on the aromas emanating from a modest shack by the path leading away from the beach. Claude and Brice bring me to a halt downwind. My nostrils quiver with pleasure as they inhale a robust odour – intoxicating to me, but one that most mortals cannot abide. 'Ooh!' says a disgusted voice behind me, 'What a stench of grease!' But I will never tire of the smell of frying potatoes.*[4]

I hope I do not have to face such a situation, but I also hope that I become increasingly able to live from what I most value. We need to start from where we are at any given time. We cannot wait for extremes. We must look at our lives as they are now – to see how we are being formed by our everyday activities. In our daily lives there is often the sense that we are doing something just to get it out of the way, so that we can get on with what we really want to do. We can even find this attitude developing towards meditation. All the time we are thinking, 'I will just get this out of the way – it's good for me – then I can get on with things.' When we have this attitude we are limiting our experience. We are placing it in a 'good for me' box.

One of the realizations we are trying to cultivate through our meditation is that life isn't really divided into distinct segments. How we do one thing will affect the mental state we take into the next. A sense of frustration and rush will stay with us. It seems all too easy for modern life to become one continuous rush tainted with frustration and a feeling that there is never enough time to do anything with care and sensitivity. So it is a very useful practice just to take one's time. The truth is that if we can take pleasure in what we do and be mindful, we will find we have more time. Our relationship with time itself can change. Time becomes full of life rather than second by second stealing our life away.

In practical terms, we might not have very much time to meditate, but we should still learn to take our time and be fully in the time that we do have. We should not rush into the meditation but take care in laying out our cushion and making sure we are comfortable. We need to prepare for the meditation, being aware of our body and taking time to tune in to how we feel. It doesn't matter if this means we spend more time in preparation than formal practice. If our approach to preparation is one of care and attention, there is no difference between that and the meditation itself. If we can find joy in placing a cushion mindfully on a mat that we have carefully smoothed out, we will find that we are in time and the time that we do have will be useful.

Shunryu Suzuki has a passage in his book of essays *Zen Mind, Beginners Mind* (a book in which I have found much joy and inspiration) that has always intrigued me:

> *So when you practise zazen [meditation], your mind should be concentrated on your breathing. This kind of activity is the fundamental activity of the universal being.*

I understand Suzuki to mean, at least in part, that when we do anything, no matter what, with clear awareness and a sense of care and kindness, we express what is highest in us. We are in the best sense most fully ourselves. There seems to me great hope in the fact that such expression can be found in the activities of our daily lives.

reflection: Witnessing Yourself

Take up your sitting posture. Spend a little time becoming aware of your body and developing a sense of your general emotional and mental state. This does not mean that you have to work out why you feel as you do; it is more a matter of just being aware of your emotional colour and state of mind. Once you feel you have settled you can begin with the first stage of the Metta Bhavana meditation (see Appendix), and cultivate a sense of kindness towards yourself.

When you have established a basis of metta towards yourself, bring to mind a situation about which you still have confused emotions. This could be something that has happened recently or from way back. It might, for example, be an occasion when you behaved harshly towards someone, while another aspect of you feels that they had it coming. Or it might be related to how somebody has acted towards you. The important thing is that you are aware of having conflicting feelings around the incident.

Rather than getting into an internal debate with yourself, give each side a few minutes to state their case, or, more importantly, let yourself experience both sides in turn. Allow yourself to be receptive to whichever side is speaking, while as far as possible avoiding the voice that wants to say 'yes but …'. What is important to note is that I am not asking you to judge which of your emotional responses is 'right', but that you let the two, or more, sides have their say.

So there is another part of you which is willing to listen to the conflicting voices without feeling the need to value one above the other. This kind of awareness is sometimes called witness awareness, and it is a type of awareness that can be developed through meditation. So in this reflection, we are not trying to make a judgement about what is the right way to feel, but simply giving all sides a chance to be experienced as fully as possible. After you feel you have given voice to the various aspects of your emotions return to the Metta Bhavana and spend a few minutes re-establishing a sense of well-wishing towards yourself, that is, try to cultivate a sense of kindness towards yourself as you are, with sometimes conflicting emotions, rather than a idealized version of yourself.

Note that I am not implying we should value all our emotions in the same way. There are many emotions we should not allow to become the basis for action. But this does not mean that it is healthy or useful to pretend they do not exist. Meditation is a place where we can develop the ability to witness ourselves fully while understanding that there is a difference between experiencing and expressing.

reflection: Appreciating Yourself

Start as always by taking a little time over your posture and making sure you are settled and have a sense of how you are. Just be aware of the breath coming and going in your body. See if you can locate a pleasurable sensation associated with your breathing. It might be quite subtle, a gentle movement in your belly for example.

Give your attention to this sensation. Don't try to make anything happen; just use this simple sensation as the focus. If you realize you mind has drifted off, bring it back to the sensation. Once you feel you have centred yourself in your body, slowly start to bring your surroundings to mind.

Bear in mind that the space you sit in is not empty, but that you sit in a space full of the element air. Without opening your eyes become aware of your surroundings. Be aware not only of the objects in the room, but also of the materials from which these objects are made. Develop a sense that everything around you has, in one way or another, been made from materials found in the natural world. Think of the brick or wood of which the building is constructed.

Become aware that even in the heart of the city the element earth is under the buildings. Let your awareness of your context slowly expand. Keeping a sense of yourself, let your imagination come into contact with the world around you. Be aware of the life that, even in an urban environment, manages to flourish: the birds, insects, plants, then beyond the town into the countryside to the ocean. Have a sense of the abundance of life, a sense of the richness of the organic and inorganic world.

Sitting quietly in the midst of all this life, encourage an awareness of being part of this world, part of the manifestation of life. Feel that you are breathing in this world, in the middle of a breathing world. Be aware that you are made of the same basic elements that make up everything around you. See if you can encourage a sense of yourself as part of this remarkable phenomenon of life. Just sit quietly for a while, having a sense of your place in the world of things.

reflection: Being in Time

Find ways of being in time, rather than against time. Take a leisurely stroll around the park; have a day in the country; sit down and listen to your favourite CD; spend an hour reading poetry.

Try to build into your daily life activities that you engage in for their own sake. Give yourself over to these simple pleasures as fully as possible. Make some time in your life free from striving and doing.

There are many activities supportive of the spiritual life, activities that create a sense of spaciousness. Just sitting with an awareness of my breath encourages a sense in me that I am in time. Feeling the breath coming and going in my body nourishes a sense of belonging to a living world unfolding within organic time. Try using awareness of your breath to slow down whenever life begins to overwhelm you. Even if you don't have time for a formal session of meditation, you can just be aware of your breath for a few minutes. Imagine as you breathe out that you are letting go of any mental tension. See if you can develop a sense of the world around you based in a feeling of kindness towards others, as if you are breathing out kindness into the world. Let your breathing be easy and relaxed, tuning in to its rhythm, feeling time in your own body.

Try to be aware if your experience begins to take on a frantic edge, when you start to feel oppressed by time. If this happens, consciously slow down. Stop for a few moments and be aware of the breath until it becomes calm.

four

BARING THE SOUL

The Imagination

I want to begin this chapter by introducing some themes I often return to, and which I touch on in other essays in this book. In particular, I am concerned with the nature and role of the imagination within a 'spiritual' life and the importance of the imagination to the 'depth', or what we could perhaps loosely term the 'soul', of the individual. I also want to touch on the nature of wisdom, where it is to be sought, and how it might find expression in our lives. My method is perhaps more suggestive than descriptive, which seems to me to be in harmony with the areas of the imagination and wisdom as the emotional basis for spiritual practice. Let us then begin with a poem:

> In it there is a space-ship
> and a project
> for doing away with piano lessons.

And there is
Noah's ark,
which shall be first.

And there is
an entirely new bird,
an entirely new hare,
an entirely new bumble-bee.

There is a river
that flows upwards.

There is a multiplication table.

There is anti-matter.

And it just cannot be trimmed.

I believe
that only what cannot be trimmed
is a head.

There is much promise
in the circumstance
. that so many people have heads.

'A Boy's Head', Miroslav Holub (trans. George Theiner)

I very much like this poem. It is very direct. It is about men, or at least boys who grow up (or perhaps down) to be men. It also forms a simple invocation to the inventiveness and imagination of a boy. The boy is not a young Einstein or Edison; he is a normal kid. The poem . is about the unlimited imagination we all had as kids. Of course the sad thing, the tragic thing, is that many of us do get trimmed. We all start off with real heads full of space and imagination, but slowly, somewhere along the path that we call growing up, our heads get trimmed. We become caught up in the doings of this world, the realities of adult life, and we get cut down to size.

The size we end up is often rather small. Many of us get buried under our lives. We are left with just our heads poking out of the sand. We find ourselves rather cut off from the feeling aspects of ourselves and bereft of a real sense of purpose. Growing up often seems to mean losing what is most alive in us, losing the sense of imagination that connects us to our lives and to the world.

At the heart of the spiritual life is a desire to regain or re-encounter this kind of imagination. We intuitively know it is not completely lost; it is still there somewhere. This desire to reconnect with the imagination, then, is one aim of the spiritual life. I am not saying that we need – or should – become children again. We can't. We have left that garden and cannot return. But to develop as individuals implies not just becoming a fully functioning adult, but also being an adult who has imagination and feeling, someone alive to both the inner and the outer worlds. Without imagination the world loses its mystery and sense of depth in which we can find meaning.

The imagination is the faculty by which activity becomes experience. Without imagination, activity just happens to us, we feel disconnected from it, as if we were separate from everything else. It is the imagination that connects us to the other and to our own lives. In the sense that I am trying to evoke, the imagination is not a flight of fancy that takes us away from the world, but a state of being fully *in* the world, feeling that the world is part of oneself, and the self part of the world. As a child, our life is one of simplicity and directness – we are entranced by the world. The whole of us responds to it. We want to know what it feels like, how it smells, how it tastes.

Often we crave nature. If we live in a city, our world can easily appear to be made up of straight lines, hard surfaces, 'dead' materials; there is a mechanical rush, everything is moving and flickering. Perhaps we sometimes go to the park or take a trip into the country, but this is not always possible.

Living Life Fully

When our imagination fails, our connection to our lives becomes brittle and our lives lack the moisture of emotion and creativity. Without the moistening of the imagination we dry up. Many people are drawn to meditation and other spiritual practices because they sense this drying up of the imagination. They have begun to feel at a loss in their own lives. We can perhaps see this as a lack of meaning – a lack of meaning that stems from losing contact with the deeper aspects of ourselves, particularly our imagination. Without the imagination the world is a dull place. Our relationships become superficial and bring us little joy. When the imagination is alive the world has colour and vibrancy. This intensity of being in the world is conjured up by figures such as Ryokan, the eighteenth-century Japanese Buddhist hermit and poet:

> First days of spring – blue sky, bright sun.
> Everything is gradually becoming fresh and green.
> Carrying my bowl, I walk slowly to the village.
> The children, surprised to see me,
> joyfully crowd about, bringing
> My begging trip to an end at the temple gate.
> I place my bowl on top of a white rock and
> Hang my sack from the branch of a tree.
> Here we play with the wild grasses and throw a ball.

For a time, I play catch while the children sing;
Then it is my turn.
Playing like this, here and there, I have forgotten the time.
Passers-by point and laugh at me, asking,
'What is the reason for such foolishness?'
No answer I give, only a deep bow;
Even if I replied, they would not understand.
Look around! There is nothing besides this.

   Ryokan (trans. John Stevens)

Ryokan led a very simple life. He often had little to eat. He meditated, played *go* with his friends, and sometimes got drunk with them. He wrote poetry, played with the village children – often forgetting his begging round – and enjoyed the beauty of the world around him. It is easy for us to dismiss his life as that of an eccentric. We might even think his life was wasted, unproductive, and lazy. Yet he is regarded with great affection in Japan, and his life and poetry have brought inspiration and delight to thousands. When we read his poetry we begin to sense that this was someone who lived his life to the full, who stepped into life completely, free from all pretensions and with a heart truly open to others and the world around him. The poem is full of joy, but many of his poems are very sad. They are sad in the same way as this one is joyful – very directly:

Alone, wandering through the mountains,
I come across an abandoned hermitage.
The walls have crumbled, and there is only a path for foxes
   and rabbits.
The well, next to an ancient bamboo grove, is dry.
Spider webs cover a forgotten book of poems that lies

beneath a window.
Dust is piled on the floor,
The stairway is completely hidden by the wild fall grasses.
Crickets, disturbed by my unexpected visit, shriek.
Looking up, I see the setting sun — unbearable loneliness.

Ryokan (trans. John Stevens)

So you have this crazy old monk, sometimes sad, sometimes happy.
There is great depth in his simple verses and poetic craft. He blends
a mature skill with a free imagination. His poems are never contrived
or artificial. What stands out is their authenticity. Ryokan lives the
simple life, the life of a hermit, but he is very connected to the world,
to life, to all around him. Sometimes he is full of joy, sometimes full
of sorrow, above all he is full of life and, in life, such feelings are very
natural. When people see him playing with children they nudge each
other. They see him as a foolish old man, wasting his life. Ryokan
responds to the ridicule of others not in words but by bowing deeply.
He does not try to explain or justify himself. He responds to the world
and others with emotional freedom, with an imagination that includes
rather than excludes life. His relationship to the world is direct — he
loses himself in play and finds himself overcome with sadness. For
Ryokan it seems that to live is to be in life. When he says, 'Look
around! There is nothing besides this,' he is suggesting that much of
the time we miss life; we fail to see what is in front of us, fail to see
the possibilities of engaging deeply with the everydayness of our lives.
This sort of engagement requires us to look around, to see the world
with imagination.

Ryokan is not a product of anything. In his essence, he is just who
he is. He has a head in Holub's sense, he is not trimmed. He cannot

be explained away in the way we so often seem compelled to explain things. He is not reducible to psychology or genetics. He is Ryokan. Of course he has a history, he has genes, but the essence that shines through cannot be reduced in these ways. This is what I take Holub to mean when he talks about 'a head that cannot be trimmed'. One of the main ways in which we trim other people, or ourselves, is by seeing them as mere products, as results. We try to understand ourselves in terms of our genetics or our environment. This is the great debate, the so-called nature versus nurture debate. These factors play an important part in who and what we are, but it is surely not the case that this is all we are. This way of looking at ourselves and others is very limiting, and the part that it limits is the part that desires to be authentic, the spiritual part. I am clearly talking here not in scientific terms. Perhaps when the Human Genome Project is complete, and when psychologists and statisticians have studied enough people, we will understand the human being completely, but for me that will be the end of the life of the imagination. When we talk about people in such ways – as merely products of their biology and social forces – we miss what is most important about them.

What Does It Mean to Be Human?

What is the point of a human life? Does it have any meaning? When we explore questions like this we find little wisdom in the social or physical sciences. What we encounter there is information. Our age has the moniker 'information age'. We have information circling the earth at the speed of light, but does it help answer these fundamental questions?

If we go back to the root of the word 'educate', we find it has its history in 'to care', and when we read the poems of Ryokan we feel this aspect of education. We have a sense of his care, a caring that flows naturally from a deep feeling for the world. This kind of care seems to embody a type of wisdom that has nothing to do with information or knowledge in its restricted sense. We do not need to know why the sun sets to be moved by it. Our connection to the world is not through information about it, but through a sense of wonder. How long is it since we have imagined an entirely new bird? How long since the cry of insects and the sight of the setting sun brought us deeply into ourselves?

For our lives to have meaning we have to be in relationship with them. Meaning comes through a depth of connection to ourselves and the world. Such a connection can exist only when we allow the imagination room. For many of us there is little room for the imagination, rather are we full of information and ideas. Imagination has traditionally been seen as a force that works through us. For the Greeks it was one of the nine goddesses, protectors of the arts and sciences – the muses. The symbol of the muse tells us that we do not own the imagination, it is not something we can control and use as we please. Instead, the muse uses us to express herself. All children seem to attract the muses. They come in play. They come bestowing a sense of wonder at the world.

The muses are normally associated with a creative endeavour – but perhaps our idea of creativity has become rather restricted. We do not have to be a painter or a poet to be creative. We can be creative in terms of being in a feeling relationship to ourselves and those around us. When we are in such a relationship we are moved by the world we live in. This is rather different perhaps from self-expression, for it relates to the self in its broadest sense. Such a capacity can no longer be regarded as 'mine', but bestows on us a sense of belonging. It is a self-awareness that includes, through the imagination, a sense of the collective self, a sense of what we have in common with the rest of life. What is expressed is both personal and transpersonal; we act and feel beyond the limited demands of the ego. Conversely, if we lose contact with the imagination we also lose the depth of awareness that is essential for a feeling of empathy and kindness towards others.

Within the Buddhist tradition this awareness is expressed through the concept of the *bodhicitta* – a term that can be translated as enlightened heart or mind. Such a heart cannot be regarded as belonging to one individual, but as a heart that is in a feeling relationship to all reality. Again, there is this sense that the bodhicitta works *through* one rather than being the property of an individual. A feeling of separation from others, and from the deeper parts of our own being, is the great tragedy of human life. In primitive cultures this state of alienation is sometimes referred to as a loss of soul. Our connection with soul has dried up. When this happens the individual is regarded as outside the community – no longer fully human. It as if we are just going through the motions. There is no sense of joy, and little feeling. The soul, in this sense, is the aspect of the psyche that keeps us in a meaningful relationship with life. Images of Ryokan playing ball with the village children or finding tears filling his eyes as he contemplates a sunset have this sense of soul. Ryokan can enter the world of a child and find simple joy, or he can be deeply moved by the natural beauty of the world. His imagination saturates his being, giving a sense of emotion and depth.

Finding Our Way Again

What can we do when our lives have dried up? There are many ways in which we can begin to encourage and strengthen a richer sense of being alive and in life. Most importantly take the time to notice, to feel, what is happening.

There is not, I think, a formulaic way to permeate the soul, to reconnect with a life that has lost its sense of meaning. We should perhaps be rather wary of methods and techniques. Of course, such things as meditation can be a great help; to set aside time to be with oneself more fully is very worthwhile. However, it is all too easy for such activities to become dry and just another thing we do. I have listened to many people complaining that their meditation no longer feels alive, that they feel they are just going through the motions. When we read books on meditation it all sounds so great, we have this idea that meditation is going to put everything right, that soon we will be free of all our problems. But it is not really like that, there is no system out there that is just going to put everything right. I am not saying there is not a lot of wisdom and support to be found in spiritual systems, but that it is all too easy for this wisdom to be treated as information that we can apply to our lives and make everything better.

Wisdom is not something that can just be taken on superficially; it has to be fully lived. It is a little like mistaking a map for the world itself. A map, however good, is just a map. Even if we do not mistake the map for the real thing, as we often do – even if we know it is just a map – we need to remember that it is never completely accurate, never fully up to date. When we get out our map to go for a walk, we often find a footpath is overgrown, a new housing estate has been built, a chalk cliff crumbled. So the map is a static thing, relating to the real world which is dynamic. But many of us never even get to the point of taking a walk at all. We just like studying the maps. We make a fetish of them but never quite go on the hike, never get to see if the map is accurate. Or we venture out and when the world does not conform to the map, we think, 'Oh dear, the world is wrong!' We imagine there is something wrong with the world because is not like the map. So we don't throw the map away or alter it; we fall back to studying the map. Perhaps the maps we have of ourselves are like this – they never fully capture all of us.

Just as a map can only exist in relation to its actual territory, wisdom needs an individual through which to express itself; it cannot exist outside an individual. It needs a real flesh-and-blood person through which to express itself. And wisdom can only express itself through someone who is alive to themselves and the world. Reading about wisdom, even meditating without imagination, is not the same as taking a walk and really looking around. Being alive to ourselves does not mean putting everything right, having everything sorted out, knowing exactly where you are going and what you will find. Rather, it is a state of openness that allows us to be surprised by our own response to the world. This openness is found more often in a state of not knowing than one of knowing. Emotionally it is a sense of being responsive to our own feelings; being open-hearted. This open-heartedness is an openness to ourselves as much as to others, it is a taking care of ourselves in the sense of allowing the heart to have its say. It is a state of being that is difficult to maintain as it means we have to allow for the complexity of feeling, and we have to make room for all of ourselves.

In another poem, Holub talks about the nature of the heart:

Officially the heart
is oblong, muscular,
and filled with longing.

But anyone who has painted the heart knows
that it is also

spiked like a star
and sometimes bedraggled
like a stray dog at night
and sometimes powerful
like an archangel's drum.

And sometimes cube-shaped
like a draughtman's dream
and sometimes gaily round
like a ball in a net.

And sometimes like a thin line
and sometimes like an explosion.

And in it is
only a river,
a weir
and at most one little fish
by no means golden.

More like a grey
jealous
loach.

It certainly isn't noticeable
at first sight.

Anyone who has painted the heart knows
that first he had to
discard his spectacles,
his mirror,
throw away his fine-point pencil
and carbon paper

and for a long while
walk
outside.[5]

'What the heart is like', Miroslav Holub

What the Heart Is Like

This poem at first seems a fairly straightforward invocation of the multifaceted character of the heart. It then takes an unexpected twist when it introduces the image of the loach. A loach is a small freshwater fish with spikes around its mouth, and is related to the carp. This might seem like a negative image. We probably have a rather more glorious idea about what is at the very heart of ourselves. But this image has the effect of pulling us up. It stops us becoming carried away with an idealized idea of ourselves. This little grey fish perhaps represents that which is vulnerable in us, that which has been disregarded, overlooked. Perhaps the loach is the neglected imagination that keeps the heart alive to itself.

When we start to look deeper into our own nature we are always confronted with paradox. At the very centre is not something grand and magnificent but something rather grey and guarded, something unknown and neglected. This is how it is for most of us. The imagination has been trimmed.

We think we know ourselves and others. We might feel that we have quite a sophisticated idea about the world. Perhaps we have read the books and studied the maps. We know how things are and why they are like they are. But we have forgotten that there is this jealous grey loach. It is perhaps with the rediscovery of this little fish trapped as it is behind the spikes of a weir that a real moistening, a real coming into life, can begin. It might be that to be alive to ourselves we have to recognize this jealous little fish. Perhaps it is jealous because it feels the need to protect itself from everything which would rather it did not exist. It has to be jealous because it wants to protect itself. It is jealous of its true nature. Paradoxically perhaps, the loach, this small, insignificant little fish with spikes around its mouth, corresponds to the bodhicitta, the great overflowing heart of a spiritual hero.

A weir is a kind of dam. It can also mean a fence of spikes set up to catch fish. Over the weir is life, the whole great river of life. This little grey fish has somehow to make it over the weir into that great stream of life, of being, of death. This is the work of the spiritual life and there is no map for this journey. Even in the great spiritual tradition of Buddhism there is no map that can show you how to leap. The map for this is somewhere in our own imagination, somewhere in the untrimmed part of us.

To make this leap means to bring the grey jealous part of ourselves into awareness, where it can assume its fullness. To do that we need fearlessness, confidence, or faith. True faith, then, has to include even those parts of us that we would rather not see, and the parts we would like to remain hidden. For the loach to make its leap we have to go into the heart, paint the heart, we need to grow down into the heart.

Most spiritual traditions, certainly in their populist modern forms, show us maps of ascension, designed with the heights in mind. They are about how to grow up and become more. They are concerned with the visible parts of ourselves. But for the poor little loach there is no map. It just has to take a chance and by a supreme act of imagination get over the weir into life. It is a kind of turning inside-out of what is most secret, most jealous, deepest within us – turning it out to face the world.

Of course this is just one side of the coin. We should not forget the bodhicitta is also like the voice of Mahalia Jackson screaming through the ether. This immense golden power streaming down with unstoppable force – we should not forget this side. The great devotional texts of the Mahayana bring this to light, but the Mahayana is still conscious of the loach. In one of the greatest Mahayana scriptures, the *Holy Teaching of Vimalakirti*, we read:

> *Flowers like the blue lotus, the red lotus, the white lotus, the water lily, and the moon lily do not grow on the dry ground in the wilderness, but do grow in the swamps and mud banks. Just so, the Buddha-qualities do not grow in living beings certainly destined for the uncreated [i.e., Enlightenment] but do grow in those living beings who are like swamps and mud banks of passions. Likewise, as seeds do not grow in the sky but do grow in the earth, so the Buddha-qualities do not grow in those determined for the absolute but do grow in those who conceive the spirit of enlightenment, after having produced a Sumeru-like mountain of egoistic views.* [6]

Painting the Heart

Buddhism can encourage in us a vision of what we can become. It can inspire us to make the effort necessary for real, positive change – to bare our soul. It provides a detailed description of the territory we need to cross. Buddhism, however, is not something outside of us. It becomes useful only if we can relate it to our own, felt, experience. We can only develop from how we actually are. To grow up into our potential also implies a growing down into our depth. This growing down takes to heart not just the spiritual aspects of ourselves but also those aspects that are often overlooked and regarded as negative.

Spiritual practice cannot then ignore the darker parts of ourselves. The meditator needs to look with compassion into the depths of the heart, and find what has been neglected and hidden away. Perhaps we will be surprised that the very things we have disregarded and hidden in the mud can, when cared for and led out, prove to have the ability to moisten, and bring new life to, the imagination.

> Anyone who has painted the heart knows
> that first he had to
> discard his spectacles,
> his mirror,
> throw away his fine-point pencil
> and carbon paper
>
> and for a long while
> walk
> outside.

Meditation, and the experiences and insights that its practice can bring, are experiences of intimacy; through spiritual practice we come into closer contact with ourselves. What we are — in all our heights and depths, in our passions and sorrows — is the soil from which we grow. What is deepest in us is perhaps never to be fully understood, nor can it be explained or analysed away, and does not appear on any spiritual, psychological, or genetic map. We can know it only in an intuitive, felt way. It is the untrimmed part of us, the imagination, the passion of our hearts and minds. The spiritual life is a coming into ourselves, a bringing to our experience of awareness and compassion. It is through a warm, clear intimacy with who we really are that a compassionate and understanding attitude towards others can develop. It is through the cherishing of our uniqueness that we realize our interconnectedness with life. When we learn to paint our heart, we give the loach the courage and confidence that it needs to jump the weir.

reflection: A Sense of Wonder

Observe nature close up. Tend a few houseplants, for example, or put fruit on view; have some onions hanging in the kitchen, and use fresh herbs.

Spend five minutes looking at a house plant. Get close up to it so that it fills your field of vision. Get comfortable, breathe, and just look. Get even closer, really study a single leaf – the tip of the leaf. Notice the colour of the plant; it's not just one green, but a number of shades and gradations. Gently touch a leaf, a stem, and feel its texture. Breathe the plant as the plant in its own way breathes you.

I still remember that every year at primary school we would grow a hyacinth bulb in a clear vase elegantly shaped for the purpose, and how the roots would grow down brown and white into the clear water. How the bulb would swell and open, at first revealing a tender sliver of green. Over the days and weeks a beautiful flower would slowly appear, as though it was a flame in a world that was slow afire with the seasons.

Create a modest jungle in your home. Even one plant can be a rainforest if you get close enough to it. Let the smells and tastes of nature be in your home. Notice what is already there. Instead of getting depressed at the harshness of the city, find its hidden nature: moss growing on a wall, weeds through the pavements, a cat moving through the gardens like a tiger in the forest.

reflection: Everyday Awareness

Turn off the television, sit quietly, and just be aware how you feel. Let the rushing that seems to fill every waking moment stop, and allow a sense of space into your life. When you do some everyday activity try to give yourself to it as fully as possible.

When you wash your hands be aware how the water feels against your skin, of the texture of the towel, the warmth or cold of the hands. When you prepare a meal feel the weight of the knife you are using to cut the vegetables. Notice the texture of the handle in your hand. Be aware of the food you are using, its colour and its smell. Prepare the meal with care.

Even if you have a very busy life, select one everyday activity and decide to do it with a little more care and attention. It might be something as ordinary as getting ready for bed. Notice, for example, the feel of buttons against your fingertips, the texture of your clothes. Perhaps get into the habit of folding your clothes neatly.

Find small ways to slow down a little, try to cultivate a sense of paying real attention to some of your everyday activities. Just do these a little slower than usual, perhaps taking a couple of aware breaths before you begin. In this way, bring a sense of mindfulness into your life. Let the mind be full of the rich yet simple activities of your life, at least now and then.

five

BEYOND BELIEF

Many of the teachings of Buddhism come down to us in the form of parables and stories. We find the extensive use of these devices in most, if not all, spiritual traditions. A story or parable will tend to engage our imagination far more than a list of rules or a highly systematized presentation. The fact that stories and parables play such a prominent part in communicating spiritual ideas also tells us something very important about the nature of those ideas. It shows us that they are not just abstract but relate directly to life. They give the teachings a human face. They also help us not to over-literalize the teachings, for parables and stories are to some degree open, they can be understood in different ways and on various levels. They are suggestive rather than precise, and push us towards further contemplation and thought.

One of the best-known of all Buddhist parables is that of the raft. It concerns a man living in a terrifying land, a land full of horror and danger. He is fleeing this land, knowing that on the other side of a vast expanse of water there lies a land of peace and love. On arriving on the shore he has to find a way to cross the water, so he builds a raft, a crude structure constructed from whatever is to hand, and with great effort eventually makes it across the water to freedom.[7]

This simple parable is rich in symbolism. Most striking, perhaps, is the water, which often appears in stories and dreams. Water is often understood as representing the psyche, in particular the unconscious. However, the Buddha seems to have a more particular point he wishes to make, for after telling the parable he asks the listeners a number of questions. The Buddha wants to know if, having completed such a journey, it would then be proper for the man to strap the raft to himself and take it wherever he went. The Buddha often seems to have conducted his teachings in the form of a dialogue. When he receives the answer that it would not be proper to carry the raft, he poses a second question. Should the man moor the raft and, unencumbered, continue on his way? To this question his fellows, a group of monks, reply 'Indeed! That would be the best course for him.'

Thus the Buddha gives the monks the highest of his teachings, then encourages them to understand it as something to be let go when the time is ripe. No other teacher warns so rigorously against dependence on his teachings, beyond believing in just his words. It seems quite clear that the Buddha is saying that the importance of a teaching lies in its usefulness – not as an article of dogma.

This is one of the most significant aspects of the Buddhist tradition. Elsewhere in the scriptures the Buddha refers to his teachings as being like the great ocean in that they all have one taste. Just as the mighty ocean everywhere has the taste of salt, so his teachings have one taste, the taste of freedom. The analogy to taste is an interesting one, for taste involves taking something into ourselves. Our reaction to taste is very direct and visceral, we know intuitively, rather than intellectually, whether or not we find it pleasant. So the

Buddha might be implying that his teachings have to be taken into the body and that the intuition rather than the intellect is to be trusted. The analogy also implies that the teachings are vast and deep like the ocean, and cannot be fathomed by the intellect.

The Taste of Freedom

So the taste the Buddha attributes to his teachings is that of freedom. But what does freedom taste like? Freedom has two sides: a freedom from and a freedom to. In the parable of the raft, someone escapes from what is oppressive to a more positive state. Buddhism is often regarded as a path leading away from suffering towards freedom from suffering, a state symbolized as Enlightenment or Nirvana.

Many things can oppress us, but perhaps more than anything we are oppressed by death. The spectre of death haunts us all: our own death, the death of those we love, the death of an enemy, the death of a pet, the countless deaths of the past, countless deaths to come, the death of love or hope.

Death is an extreme form of change. Change, the impermanence of all conditioned things, is the central teaching of the Buddha. The characteristic that marks all existence is the never-ending process of change. It is not that 'things' change, but that the essential quality of things *is* change. Whenever we forget this most basic characteristic of reality we become vulnerable to suffering. What Buddhism seems to be offering is a method of practice and ethics that brings us into full realization and alignment with the basic characteristic of reality, its impermanence.

Buddhism teaches that our fear of death is to be found in our relationship to life, and that this fear has to be faced up to and integrated into our lives. It is because we constantly expect and desire life to be permanent that death so haunts us. We often feel betrayed by life: that people have let us down, that life is unfair. We become increasingly wary of life, holding ourselves back because we fear that disappointment will follow if we give ourselves fully to life. We live in a state of anxiety, worried that we will lose what we have, that disappointments lurk around each corner. The aim of Buddhism is to free us from this anxiety, but for this to happen we have to undergo a profound transformation, we have to come to terms with impermanence; more than come to terms with it, we have to experience impermanence within our own being, realizing on a deep emotional level that this is our very essence. We are not dealing with metaphysics here. There is no theology involved. The taste of freedom is the taste of impermanence. When we come to the experience of impermanence as not just out there, but in here, in our very nature, we can move beyond the clinging that causes us so much pain, disappointment, and anxiety. The other shore is to be found.

It is this deepening understanding of the nature of our own experience, through the cultivation of awareness, that is the central practice of Buddhism. Buddhism shows that we are not free, but driven by fears, anxieties, and influences of which we are only dimly aware. Many of us have a naïve idea of free will; we believe that we just have it. We do not understand that such qualities have to be cultivated and nurtured. Consider our behaviour in relation to the democratic process, seen in the West as the ultimate expression of free will. The most reliable predictor of a vote is the voting behaviour of the parents of the voters. The conditions that influence our exercise of this 'ultimate freedom' have little to do with freedom of thought, but are largely a consequence of our family and social contexts. This action, which in the West is the symbol of the exercise of free will, is for most of us little more that a reaction of habits and prejudices we have inherited from others.

Loosening our Beliefs

If we begin to look clearly at our lives we find that most of what we do, even how we feel, just happens to us. There is little real self-reflection, scant understanding of the habits and unconscious forces that underlie our actions. In a sense, we suffer from a lack of imagination, in that it is through imagination that we connect more deeply with ourselves. For many, the imagination, which is flexible and inventive, has been replaced by fixed ideas and habits. For the imagination to reawaken there has to be a loosening of these habits, a letting go of old ideas about ourselves and the world. Some things have to be dropped to enable others to arise.

In the Buddhist tradition the spiritual life starts with renunciation. This recalls the Buddha's own going forth into the homeless life. We often understand this as a going forth from an opulent lifestyle to a simpler one, but it is far more an internal going forth than an external one, though the external might be necessary. While the external going forth is a movement away from material dependence, the internal going forth is a movement away from fixed beliefs and ideas. The well-known Zen story of the inflated scholar and Zen master reminds us of this:

◆ ◆ ◆

A UNIVERSITY PROFESSOR is visiting a Zen master. When the master comes to pour the professor his tea, once the cup is full he just keeps pouring. The tea overflows onto the low table, then on to the tatami mats on the floor. But he keeps pouring until the teapot is empty. The professor has been given all the tea, but his full cup can hold no more. Most of us are already full of unexamined ideas and undigested beliefs. The going forth is an emptying of ourselves, a making room.[8]

◆◆◆

We can see meditation in this light. The simple practice of just sitting with the breath and taking notice of our mind and body is a way of beginning to empty ourselves. When we sit, all sorts of fantasies, fears, and anxieties arise. We can learn to watch them with a kind and open awareness. We watch them rise and fall away. So when we meditate we should be content just to watch what is taking place. If we can do this, we begin to have a sense that most of what goes on is unnecessary; it can just be observed and let go of. We start to see how we construct elaborate and unnecessary complexes around our experience.

A simple example might be when we feel a little discomfort when we sit for meditation. We soon find ourselves in a terrible mental state. It's just a small sensation in our leg but we become desperate to get up. We start resenting the meditation teacher for making us sit, we begin to feel this whole meditation thing is a waste of time. But sometimes we are able to let go of all of that and return to the sensation. If it is observed in a clear and kind way it will usually pass and give way to another sensation. In time we strengthen our ability to sit with our experience in a simple and direct way. We also find that outside meditation we seem to have less need to over-complicate our experience. We might find that we seem to be thinking less; the constant chatter, fuelled by craving and anxiety, very slowly diminishes.

If we manage to let go of something, we should not be in a hurry to replace it with something else. Many of us only let go of something when we have already picked out its replacement. We are never without. We give an old couch to our less well off friends, but not until a new one has been delivered, or we start an affair before we say goodbye to our wife or husband. We seem terrified of not having these things in our life. And the new is always seen in the light of the old. It is then not really new at all, just a new version of the old.

This kind of grasping seems to be based in fear. It is quite hard to get at the root of this fear, but it is related to over-investing in things. It is as if we believe that things makest man; our sense of self-worth is bound up with what we own and control. One of the real benefits of meditation, then, is having the experience of being content with just being.

Perhaps the hardest things to let go of are the beliefs and views we use to shore up our sense of how and what we are. But Buddhism is not about swapping one set of clothes for another, it does not ask us simply to replace our old beliefs or emotions for newer, updated versions, but to experience what it is like to let go of them, to stand naked. Clearly we cannot just shrug off our views. To do so prematurely would leave us in a state of confusion and anxiety. Nevertheless, we can try to see ourselves in a process of slowly loosening our rigid attitudes, wearing them as a suit of clothes rather than a suit of armour.

What we have to be willing to do is place our trust in our experience rather than in our ideas about our experience. That means being able to experience on a level that is relatively free from prejudice and rigid ideas.

Most of us operate from quite rigid assumptions; this kind of rigidity means we don't really bring awareness to bear. We can see an extreme of this in the political arena, how self-interest and hard ideologies operate. When two opposing politicians speak, we know beforehand what stance they will take. We are shocked and delighted on the extremely rare occasion that one of them says something that is not predictable and over-rehearsed. If one of them were to listen to and consider the other's view, we would probably think it was two actors playing at being politicians. This is a very sad state of affairs but it really isn't that different from how we all are most of the time. We take our views and beliefs as true. If we are forced to give one up, we replace it with another as soon as possible.

The next time you meet someone new, notice how quickly you impose a whole set of feelings and judgements on them. Ask yourself what basis there is for these views.

Buddhism is not offering us a tidy set of rules and beliefs in order that we can feel safe and comfortable. It is asking us to go beyond belief and examine our experience. This is the real message of the Buddha. Above the doors to Enlightenment is written 'Abandon all fear.' Entering has to be a letting go. Our fear of change has to be let go. To let go of the fear is to enter the impermanence of reality. Rumi captures the emotion of going forth:

Last night my teacher taught me the lesson of poverty:
Having nothing and wanting nothing.
I am a naked man standing inside a mine of rubies,
clothed in red silk.
I absorb the shining and now I see the ocean,
billions of simultaneous motions
moving in me.
A circle of lovely, quiet people
becomes the ring on my finger.

Then the wind and thunder of rain on the way.
I have such a teacher.

'I Have Such a Teacher', Rumi (trans. Coleman Barks)

The Right Questions

In Buddhism we have to let go of old habits, let go into our direct experience of life, stand naked, free from our rigid beliefs and views, open to our experience of ourselves. This nakedness implies openness to the world around us; we expose ourselves to the dense richness of what is all around us. We are able to absorb life, become saturated with life, full of it. The role of such a teacher, or a spiritual system of practice, is to help us stand naked and to hear the thunder of rain without fear. Such a teacher is not to be sought in a guru but in our everyday experience of life. The Buddha never offered those who came to him any mystical powers. He did not offer them some ritual or magic mantra that guarantees Enlightenment – there are no such spells. He directed them to look more closely at their actual experience. He found ways to help people bring a new level of awareness to their situations.

The Buddha gave people the courage to ask the right questions and be receptive to the answers. The questions are simple: What leads to happiness? How does my behaviour affect me? What does the best in me long for? These are simple questions but difficult to ask because the answers point towards change and the unknown, towards a letting go of the perceived norms of our world, towards stepping outside of what is expected of us. We are pointed to go beyond the unexamined beliefs that give us a sense of security and bind us to lives we find unsatisfactory. We are pointed towards a going forth. The imagination needed for change often comes from a growing dissatisfaction with our lives or a sudden upheaval.

We all come to points in our lives when things break down. This might be brought about by external events, like the death of a loved one, a broken heart, or the build-up of internal dissatisfaction. The *Bardo Thödol*, one of the central and best known Tibetan Buddhist texts, is a text read over a dead body to give guidance to the consciousness as it transmigrates from one life to next, but death is only one of our many transitions. At certain points in our lives the fabric of our normal existence comes apart. Such points, though painful and difficult, are great opportunities for change. The root verses contained in the texts offer advice and support for positive change. There are six of these verses. The fifth, known as the bardo (literally 'gap') of Reality, which comes after the bardo of death, and before the bardo of rebirth, begins:

> O now, when the Bardo of Reality upon me is dawning,
> Abandoning all awe, fear, and terror of all (phenomena),
> May I recognize whatever appeareth as being mine own
>   thought-forms,
> May I know them to be apparitions in the Intermediate
>   State;
> (It hath been said) 'There arriveth a time when the chief
>   turning-point is reached;
> Fear not the bands of the Peaceful and Wrathful, Who are
>   thine own thought-forms.

> trans. Lama Kazi Dawa-Samdup

This might at first reading appear a rather esoteric piece of advice, but in essence it is very simple. 'Bardo' can imply a state in which, for whatever reason, our normally tight hold on our 'reality' has loosened. A common response to this 'gap' is fear, a desire to cling tenaciously to what we know – normal service to be resumed as soon as possible. But such situations, though frightening, offer us a great opportunity for change. From a traditional Tibetan view, when we die we are torn away from all we hold dear. All our dreams and ideas are suddenly seen for what they are; lacking any real substance. But lesser bardos happen quite often in our lives. It might be as simple as someone pointing out a way in which our behaviour has hurt them. Even in this everyday example, we often feel a sense of insecurity because our view of ourselves is challenged. In these situations we can feel a tendency to rationalize so as to reinforce the view we have of ourselves and to feel critical of the other person. However, there is a way of just staying with the situation and not immediately shoring up our fragile egos. When we do this, we dwell for a time in a bardo, an opportunity to change, to see ourselves more as we really are rather than our elaborately constructed sense of self. This is what Buddhism is asking us to do; to cling less to our ideas and beliefs and to take notice of the experience of our life as it happens. To do this means that we make possible new and creative responses to life.

Rubbing Up Against Reality

Spiritual development means learning to see that our whole life can become the ground for practice. The teachings of the bardos refer to turning-points in life when extreme circumstances open up the possibility to radically shift our self-view. These are times when Reality impinges strongly on the self-centred 'reality' of the ego. Such times might lead us into depression; we might seek the support of tranquil-lizers or find other means to take the edge off our experience. Yet it is at times like this that our meditation practice can prove its worth. The loosening up of the ego that such a practice can help to foster makes it easier to use the opportunities that life throws at us. If we have learned to sit with ourselves, and experienced more deeply the way the mind works, we will be less thrown by circumstance. The less ego-bound our experience, the more open we are to change.

The beautiful terms employed by Shunryu Suzuki, big mind and small mind, resonate again here. The idea of small mind captures the cramped and restrictive nature of our psyche when it is dominated by the ego. Nevertheless, it holds the possibility of infinite expansion, for it is itself part of big mind. Big mind conjures up the ocean or the open skies of the desert. Every situation is part of big mind. When we are in touch with big mind we find support for the changes and difficulties of life. Here there is no sense of loss. Nothing is destroyed. Big mind means we do not collapse into ourselves, feeling we're a victim of life. Nor do we desperately try to shore up the ego, through rationalization and blame. Instead, we stay open to each situation, bringing to it kindness and clarity. Such a mind needs care and cultivation. It is forever available to us. It is a finding of depth and awareness – soulfulness – within the situations in which we find ourselves. We do not need to wait until we are in desperate straits before we try to cultivate big mind, we can look for it in all our experiences.

I was recently in New England during autumn. To someone coming from England, where we have a sedate autumn, it was quite overwhelming. The season's announcement of change is a beautiful natural phenomenon. We witness the rebecoming of leaves going back to the ground. No clear distinction can be made between the trees, the ground, and leaves. Everywhere there is life intimately related. I felt time, not as divided space, but as woven strands, from the time of a forest, to the time of the wind. I was on solitary retreat and had plenty of time just to sit in the woods. The glorious display of change also had a certain melancholic element to it. It reminded me of my life passing, of losses I had suffered. It was a time in which I could reflect on impermanence, when I felt an opening out to nature, to beauty, and to change and loss. I felt my own life, its delights and sorrow, held in a broader context, that of the natural, never-ending rhythms of life. Although I was alone, I felt connected to others. I felt a sense of love towards myself and the world.

Emotionally we have to depend upon love. Love, in the sense of genuine compassion, makes the 'soul' porous, and allows a kind of saturation to occur. Love allows the ego to soften and find its connection with soul. When we are confronted with our limited self, we can bring an emotion of love to the points where we feel our limitations. We have to learn to rub up against Reality with love.

This is a kind of paying attention. We pay attention but with a sense of altruism. This is a big mind response to life: a desire to support and nurture it, to give ourselves to it. Confidence or faith consists in a giving of our limited selves to what we instinctively feel is beyond it. We give small mind to big mind. The limitations of the mind prove to be pressed against Reality itself, and it is in the friction between small mind and big mind that compassion is generated. Ryokan explains,

> If there is beauty, there must be ugliness;
> If there is right, there must be wrong.
> Wisdom and ignorance are complementary,
> And illusion and enlightenment cannot be separated.
> This is an old truth, don't think it was discovered recently.
> 'I want this, I want that'
> Is nothing but foolishness.
> I'll tell you a secret —
> 'All things are impermanent!'

reflection: Sitting with Sensation

It is within the context of our own bodies that meditation takes place, so in order to meditate effectively our attitude towards our body needs to be in harmony with the mental state we are striving to cultivate. We can use the sensations in our body themselves as the object of meditation.

When sitting to meditate, see that your body is alert and upright. Consciously relax your face and shoulders along with any other areas in which you know you tend to hold tension. You might like to imagine breathing into and through any areas of tension, using the breath to encourage a softening of the muscles and tissue.

Once you have quietened down a little, start to focus on the sensations in your body. Let the mind go to the strongest sensation. Don't try to hold on to or change the sensation; just let the mind move around the body as sensations arise and pass away. If there is a persistent sensation in one place, encourage the awareness to investigate the nature of that sensation.

Notice how that sensation is changing. Is it hot and sharp, or perhaps dull and diffuse? Does it feel twisted or compressed, stretched or compacted? Is the sensation consistent? If not, how is it changing? Rather than react to an unpleasant sensation and draw back from it, try to explore it. See if it's possible to let go of any aversion and take a interest in how it really feels.

Try not to tense up around the sensation, but consciously relax the surrounding area. You will probably find that after a while the sensations in one particular area diminish, and another area of sensation attracts the mind. So just sit and take an interest in the various sensations that arise, allowing the mind to move freely from one to another and further investigate the complex of sensation if you find the mind holding on to it.

What you are trying to do is resist, or at least go beyond, habitual reactions to sensation, so rather than just register a particular set of sensations as pleasant or unpleasant, investigate their actual make-up. You will probably find you spend more time with sensations you are inclined to regard as unpleasant or even painful than those you regard as pleasant – although both types should be regarded.

You might find when you investigate these various areas of sensation that regarding them as pleasant or unpleasant is far more arbitrary than you had thought. See if you can have a sense of the awareness being warm and kind, so just take your time to feel what is there. Of course, if the sensation is really painful you should do something about it, rather than risk damage to your body.

six

WALKING

In beauty	may I walk
All day long	may I walk
Through the returning seasons	may I walk
Beautifully will I possess again	
Beautifully birds	
Beautifully joyful birds	
On the trail marked with pollen	may I walk
With grasshoppers about my feet	may I walk
With dew about my feet	may I walk
With beauty	may I walk
With beauty before me	may I walk
With beauty behind me	may I walk
With beauty above me	may I walk
With beauty all around me	may I walk
In old age, wandering on a trail of beauty,	
lively,	may I walk

In old age, wandering on a trail of beauty,

                           living again,   may I walk

It is finished in beauty

It is finished in beauty

> 'In Beauty May I walk', from the Navajo (trans. Jerome K. Rothenberg)

Stripping Down Our Experience

When we think about meditation we naturally think in terms of sitting quietly, because sitting quietly is the simplest thing anyone can do. We are trying to strip down our experience to its fundamental elements, because by keeping our experience as simple as possible, we start to understand more clearly what it is made up of. It is a way of experiencing ourselves that is free from the complications in the rest of our lives. We enter a situation that is less conditioned by the continuous activity of our five senses investigating the outside world. When we sit still, attending to our breath, we give ourselves a chance to experience ourselves in a different way. It is not that being active is in any sense bad, but that for many of us our life is very one-sided. All our waking time is taken up by activity of one sort or another. Spending half an hour a day sitting quietly can help us to gain a better perspective on the constant activity of our lives.

Ideally, when we meditate we should do nothing at all. We just sit and pay attention to our experience as it arises and passes away. In practice this is not possible for most of us; our minds are far too active, and in no time at all we become caught up in thoughts of one kind or another, so the mind must be given some object around which it can collect. We are not trying to stop the activity of the mind; the effort could cause tension and create more disturbance. As in the classic Zen ox-herding pictures, we begin by giving the mind plenty of freedom. If we are using the breath to concentrate the mind, we gently remind ourselves that the breath is already part of our experience. It is not something we have to add on. When we sit still, the breath will gradually become the focus of our awareness, as it is now our foremost activity. This might take us some time, because we have a lot of undigested feelings and thoughts, a lot of experience that is just piled up. It is a little like coming to your desk when it is covered in papers. You might be able to push them to one side and get on with what you need to do, or you might not. In the end, though, you will have to spend some time sorting them out.

Meditation is not so much a matter of sorting things out, but letting them settle. When one puts a wild ox in a spacious field, it will charge around. Then perhaps it will stop for a while, eat a little, and start running around again. If the herder waits patiently, the ox will eventually come to him. The herder remains there as part of the situation and in time the ox, having spent its energy, will become interested. It will feel a need to make a relationship with that situation. It is like this in meditation. We need to give ourselves some time for the relationship to develop. We have to learn that the breath is not going to go away but is patiently waiting for us to notice it. Once we have formed a relationship, things get a little easier. The ox, being an ox, will still need to romp around now and then, but it will trust the herder and be happy to see him.

Even if we are quite serious about meditation it's often hard to find the time, so while it is good to meditate as much as we can, we also need to find other ways to cultivate the qualities we are trying to encourage through meditation. Sometimes the ox needs an even bigger field; it is not ready to sit down and be quiet. Walking is another means of developing mindfulness. It is a simple activity and has the great advantage of physical sensations that we can use to interest and gather the mind.

Walking Meditation

When I teach meditation I usually start with a period of walking. There are different styles of walking. Some link the steps to the pattern of the breath, but to start with I like to keep it really simple. We just walk around the room at an slow, easy pace. I give people time to take in their surroundings and begin to relax. Then I ask them to notice any sensations they feel as they place their feet on the floor. As we walk, we become interested only in what is there. We try to develop a feeling of trust in the situation so that we don't feel we have to add anything extra to it. We put down one foot and then lift the other. The sensations arise and fall away. We are not interested in hanging on to the previous sensation or anticipating the next.

Our experience of the world is often very complex. We are involved in trying to make sense of what is happening: 'What did he mean by that?' 'What is going to happen next?' When we walk as a form of meditation, we have the opportunity to let go of a lot of this confusion. We just walk. There is nowhere to get to and there is no need for anxiety. Although the situation is very simple it is also quite rich. Whenever we have a preconceived idea about what should happen, or how we should feel, we make it harder for ourselves to experience things as they really are. People are often surprised that simply walking can be so enjoyable and absorbing.

Walking is particularly effective when done with others. There is something very elemental in forming a circle and walking together. When we walk with others we have an opportunity to enter into a relationship with one another. This is also true of group meditation, but a sense of a collective practice can be more accessible when we are joined in movement. We are walking in the steps of one another, following and being followed. We can be aware of those we walk with. We can have a sense of supporting and being supported by our fellow meditators. It is difficult to express how special this can feel. The simple act of walking mindfully together can create a rich sense of collective practice. I have sometimes felt the activity of walking meditation has brought me close to experiencing what I believe the Zen master Tozan was pointing towards when he said:

> The blue mountain is the father of the white cloud. The white cloud
> is the son of the blue mountain. All day long they depend on each
> other, without being dependent on each other. The white cloud is always
> the white cloud. The blue mountain is always the blue mountain.

When we do something very simple together – like walking slowly and mindfully in a circle – we can have a sense that we are dependent on one another, yet at the same time we have a strong sense of ourselves as independent. Everyone is aware of themselves and at the same time aware of the others. If one person were to stop, or start running around and shouting, the mindful atmosphere would be broken, but each person is walking mindfully because this is what they have chosen to do. The individual effort to be aware strengthens the general atmosphere of mindfulness, and this in turn helps each individual to be more aware.

In the Seen, Only the Seen

Even if we are walking on our own we should not get lost in our own private world. We don't have to exclude our surroundings, just be aware of them in a relaxed and natural manner. We try to relax the senses, not listening or looking but letting sights and sounds come to us, open to our experience but not caught up in it. This is illustrated in a well-known story in the life of the Buddha concerning a character called Bahiya of the Bark Garment.

◆◆◆

BAHIYA IS AN ASCETIC attempting to gain Enlightenment, and he wears clothes made from bark fibres. At some point he realizes that his way of practising is not helping him, so he resolves to find a teacher, and on hearing of the Buddha he sets out to find him. On arriving at Jeta's Grove, where the Buddha is staying, he encounters a large number of monks practising walking meditation in the open air. They inform Bahiya that their master has gone to the nearby town in search of alms, so Bahiya catches up with the Buddha while he is going from house to house begging for food. Bahiya throws himself to the ground at the feet of the Buddha and cries out,

Let the exalted one teach me dhamma. Let the wellfarer teach me dhamma such as may be to my profit and happiness for a long time!

The Buddha replies,

You come unseasonably, Bahiya. We have entered in quest of alms-food.

Bahiya repeats his request and only to receive the same answer. It was the Buddha's custom that if someone asked him the same question three times, he would reply, whatever the circumstances. So when Bahiya asks for a third time the Buddha responds:

Then, Bahiya, thus must you train yourself: In the seen there will be just the seen, in the heard just the heard, in the imagined just the imagined, in the cognized just the cognized. Thus you will have no 'thereby'. That is how you must train yourself. Now, Bahiya, when in

the seen there will be to you just the seen, in the heard just the heard,
in the imagined just the imagined, in the cognized just the cognized,
then, Bahiya, as you will have no 'thereby', you will have no 'therein'.
As you, Bahiya, will have no 'therein', it follows that you will have no
'here' or 'beyond' or 'midway between'. That is just the end of Ill.

On hearing these words Bahiya gains the liberation he has
been seeking.[9]

◆◆◆

This story is interesting because it contains one of the most concise
instructions about practice to be found in the Buddhist scriptures.
Here we see the bare bones of the Buddha's teaching: be aware of
things as they are.

Normally, we have some idea how things should be, or how we
would like them to be. Such ideas stand between us and a pure
experience of how things really are. Through fear, or desire, we
reconstruct the world to make it as we would like it. In this way, much
of life is a farce. We distort the world around us in an attempt to make
it fit our egocentric and selfish views. In Hollywood romantic come-
dies all turns out well, but reality is often more like King Lear and we
end up losing our real selves.

A Sense of Care

If we perform any simple activity with a sense of care, we can come
back to what is essential in ourselves. This coming back is important
because we spend so much time away from a basic connection with
our bodies and our feelings. It is a matter of finding a balance. If we
have a busy and demanding life we need to find ways in which we can
cultivate a simple experience of contentment and joy. In modern

culture we are expected to put this off until we retire. Advertisements for retirement funds show youthful-looking pensioners taking the time, as the saying goes, to smell the flowers. However, the reality is more likely to be that after a life of frantic activity we find we have lost our sense of smell and end up feeling depressed and useless. Our sense of worth is increasingly linked to our ability to be productive and in turn to consume. It is of little importance that much of what is produced and then consumed is of no real value. That it sells is all the justification required.

Traditionally, Buddhism stresses a simple life. It doesn't do this out of some sense of asceticism, but because the more caught up we become in the commercialism of life, the further we move from a life of relatedness and joy. We do not live in a culture that supports a simple life. We are supposed to find satisfaction and happiness in products. A new car is meant to give us a feeling of freedom and potency, even if most of the time we are stuck in a traffic jam, with the vast majority of the cars having a single occupant feeling, like us, frustrated and angry.

We live in a particular culture and what we value and feel we need is to a large extent conditioned by that culture. It is important to acknowledge that we are affected by what surrounds us. A culture based in greed will incline us to be greedy, because this is acceptable, even expected behaviour. It is all too easy to feel that this is a normal and healthy way to live. The antidote to greed is not some form of self-denial, but a direct experience that greed brings not happiness but suffering. Greed makes us discontented and frustrated. The experience of finding well-being and contentment through being aware of our breath, or walking peacefully, highlights the poverty of basing our lives around accumulation and consumerism.

When I first went to San Francisco I lived right next to the ocean. I would often walk along the coastal path. It was very rare to see anyone out walking. They were all roller-blading, jogging, power walking, or cycling. No one seemed content just to walk. It was as if walking was a waste of time, that some other benefit had to be derived. The pleasure of just walking was lost. The awful expression 'multi-tasking' has become popular in recent years. It celebrates the ability to do more than one thing at a time. This idea has been extended to include the act of taking a stroll along the beach. It is no surprise, then, that when people first try to meditate they find it rather difficult.

Walking in Beauty

The beauty referred to in the poem at the start of this chapter is the beauty of feeling oneself to be part of the world rather than cut off from it. If our relationship to the world is based in exploitation and greed, it will be very hard to find any beauty. To walk in beauty means to walk with an awareness that is open and appreciative of the world around us. To be open to beauty requires us to develop an attitude of contentment rather than greed. When our lives are dominated by a feeling of inner poverty we are not able to experience beauty. Instead, we suffer from avarice and jealousy. Beauty is in the mind of the beholder; a mind full of anxiety and greed is not able to experience it. We need to find beauty in the very act of walking. It is there in the movement of the body, in the feeling of the air on our skin. When we relax into walking, allowing the simple rhythm of the body to calm us, we begin to encourage a mental state that can appreciate the world around us. We can find a quiet place, perhaps somewhere in nature, and just walk – so we are not trying to get anywhere, just walking. We just keep walking, aware of our bodies, aware of our feelings – letting them come and go, just as we let one step become the next.

Without rushing, we will in time begin to understand what it is to walk in beauty.

Walking with others it sometimes seems that the very ground we are walking on becomes charged with a sense of loving-kindness. This feeling brings me to a sense of connectedness to the earth. As we walk on the earth, encouraging a sense of care and kindness, it is as if the earth itself responds – and up through the soles of our feet we experience the sustaining nature of the earth. When such feelings stir, the act of walking becomes a ritual act. We feel ourselves participating in a calm yet joyous celebration of the earth and the life sustained by the earth. Our sense of self has been at least temporarily transformed.

At first we bring our awareness of the body into the feet. We walk with care and attention. As awareness becomes clear and flexible, it extends to include an awareness of the others we walk with. We feel a sense of appreciation to be practising with these people, a feeling of support and the wish to support them. What is between us, common to us all, is the earth on which we walk. And we walk together in the beauty of that earth. In beauty we walk.

You can bring the imagination into play as you walk. Without going off into some elaborate fantasy we can engage the imagination in a way that is related to the experience we are having. We imagine the in-breath lifting the foot and the out-breath lowering it, or just have a sense of the soles breathing. Something as simple as the thought of placing each foot with a sense of care and kindness can be very effective. I often ask what would it be like to walk with loving-kindness and invite people to bring a sense of metta into their walking. We can imagine that a footprint of kindness has been left for us to step into, and that we in turn leave an imprint of kindness for those who follow. Reflecting in this way we feel a stronger relationship to those with whom we are practising.

When you walk, try to maintain some degree of awareness of your surroundings. Although your focus is the activity of walking, you should try not to collapse into that experience, becoming tense and constricted. The tone of the mind should be clear and expansive. Fans of basketball will recognize this kind of absorption in the play of Michael Jordan, whose greatness, at least in part, lies in his ability to be totally focused, and at the same time exhibit an uncanny awareness of the whole court. Phil Jackson, the coach of the Chicago Bulls basketball team during the years that Jordan dominated the game, has an interest in meditation and sometimes called on a meditation teacher to help in his coaching.

We tend to think of concentration as excluding a broader awareness, but the two are not mutually exclusive. Through meditation, either sitting or walking, we can experience this kind of awareness. The mind is not distracted from the focus of its attention. It is undisturbed by the broader situation but not unaware of it. When the mind becomes free from anxiety and negative emotions, it becomes clear and flexible. It no longer clings to the thoughts and feelings that arise and it no longer clings to the sense impressions it experiences. Through practice, we are developing a mind that is aware and responsive but also flexible and able to let go easily. This letting go is illustrated in the well-known story of the two monks out walking who encounter a beautiful young woman.

◆ ◆ ◆

A YOUNG WOMAN in a silk kimono is standing on a road, and pondering how she will cross over some mud without ruining her finery. One of the monks offers to carry her across in his arms. This done, the two monks continue on their way.

Some time later, the other monk, no longer able to contain himself, confronts his brother, demanding to know how a monk could allow himself to carry a woman, a flagrant breach of the rules, which prohibit a monk from touching a woman. The accused monk replies, 'I put her down back there. Are you still carrying her?'[10]

◆◆◆

This story is often told to illustrate the danger of clinging to the letter of ethical behaviour while ignoring the spirit, but it also illustrates the kind of mind we are cultivating in meditation – one that can respond to the situation while not getting caught up in it. This is an aspect of walking meditation that I enjoy – the sense of movement. Not just physical movement, but allowing ourselves, with each step, to fully enter the present. We fully experience each step, stepping fully into time.

reflection: Walking I

Relax into a simple experience, like walking. As you walk, begin to enjoy the feeling of the body moving in space. Pay attention to the body, noticing all the subtle sensations. Enjoy the feeling of the feet making and breaking contact with the floor. Notice that the heel of the foot feels very different from the sole. The relative hardness of the heel contrasts with the softness of the sole. Experience your toes. Maybe you notice that you are gripping with the toes and can let them relax, allowing them to spread on the floor. Start with the soles of the feet making and breaking contact with the ground. Notice the changing sensations in the feet, then the ankles and legs, and so on.

As you walk, begin to allow the body to let go. You might notice your shoulders are high. Let them go. Maybe your face is tight. Try to soften it a little. So you are taking care of your experience, becoming aware of its richness. It is not a matter of analysing your experience, imposing some kind of control over it. It is just letting go into it. You do not have to do anything special to be aware of what is happening. The idea is to pay attention to the physical sensations in the body that arise and fall away as we move.

Keep your awareness relaxed and open. There is no need to strain. Just experience what is happening. By gently encouraging an awareness of the experience of walking, the mind can slowly drop all that is not directly concerned with the actual situation. As you let go of what is 'extra', the mind will become increasingly calm and clear. You can then stop trying to control your experience and stop trying to impose your will on the world around you.

reflection: Walking 2

To deepen concentration, try linking the steps to the breath, lifting the foot on the in-breath and placing it down on the out-breath. Make each step quite short so that the heel of the leading foot comes down level with the toes of the trailing one. This slow style of walking builds a strong awareness of the body and the breath. It is a great antidote to the frantic pace of many people's lives. At first it might feel frustrating to walk so slowly, but if you stick with it you will begin to experience a sense of calm.

Once you have accepted you are not going anywhere fast, you can find yourself becoming absorbed in the relationship you are building between the breath and the movement of the body. Although you are walking very slowly, allow the movement to be smooth. At first you might find you are tense in the shoulders, or that you are screwing up your face in concentration, but just be aware of this and encourage a soft and relaxed body. If you lose the synchronization between the breath and the steps, stop for a moment, reconnect with the breath, and start again.

There are other, even slower forms of walking meditation in which, for example, one step takes two complete breaths, but do not get too concerned about the right form – just enjoy taking the breath for a walk.

seven

UNFIXING OURSELVES

When I begin a meditation course I ask participants why they want to learn to meditate. The most common reply is that they need to calm down; they live stressful lives and hope that meditation will help them to unwind. Others have an interest in what could be termed spiritual development, but these are a small minority. It might be that people in this secular age are uncomfortable admitting to a spiritual aspiration. Even so, it seems that, on the whole, people look towards meditation mainly as a technique to help them deal with the stresses of modern life. It is interesting that meditation has this reputation, and that the supposed benefits of stress reduction have been responsible for its growing popularity. Meditation is traditionally a spiritual practice, and whatever health benefits it might confer have been seen, if at all, as secondary.

It is also probably true that only in more recent times have the physical and spiritual health of the individual been regarded as separate. Where, in the past, we might have sought reason for our disease in the territory of the soul, we now tend towards scientific explanations. Despite this, conditions like stress are not treatable with antibiotics, and meditation has become one of the officially sanctioned means with which to address such annoying complaints. I am rather uneasy about seeing meditation as a stress reduction technique, partly because this encourages an idea of meditation that strips it of its real value, and partly because I am not sure that it *is* effective in stress reduction. But my main misgiving about offering meditation as a panacea for the ills of modern life is that, in so doing, meditation is being used to address the symptoms rather than the causes of the disease. Furthermore, by mitigating the symptoms we miss out on learning some lessons about the way we live our lives.

A Productive Life?

Stress seems to be a major contributory factor to a wide variety of health problems, and has many causes. Lifestyles that produce stress in one person seem to be the conditions under which other people thrive. The manner in which most of us live leaves little room for the considerable differences in human temperaments. We are all expected to embrace the notion of an economically productive life as the rationale for life itself. Education is increasingly vocational, stressing the development of skills that will allow us to become a success in the world of work. It is presumed that by so doing the student gains access to the 'good life'. This stress on the development of economically productive skills seems to be reaching further and further back into childhood. Education as a 'leading out' of the child, the development of the imagination and ethical sensibility, have become secondary, if they are addressed at all. Only the old, who have 'earned' their leisure, seem exempt from the pressure to be productive. Even motherhood is no longer valued above work. In the United States, single mothers are now required to work in order to qualify for welfare. In a culture where family values are lauded, the idea that a woman should be 'productive' is given precedence over child-rearing, while the state offers scant provisions for childcare. The rationale of forcing mothers to work or starve seems to be that the negative effects on the child of having a welfare mum are dire. It is as if the new cause of all neuroses, replacing Freud's parental bedroom, is the actual presence of the 'unemployed' mother.

I have been shocked at the importance given to work in the United States, while the rest of life is seen as secondary. The media portrays the developed personality as one which works hard and plays hard. After twelve hours at our dot.com job we go to the gym, work out, then go to a sophisticated restaurant with our beautiful (read success-ful) counterpart. At weekends, according to this image, we 'gear up', jump in the four by four, and go for a hike. Somewhere we fit in participation in an 'extreme' sport. The stressful lifestyle is the successful lifestyle. In reality, 50% of Americans are obese, according to government health sources, while the quantity of television watched is mind boggling, as is its quality. For many, the demands of work leave them capable of little more than collapsing in front of the anaesthetizing television.

This importance of work transcends the idea of making a reason-able living. It has become the very rationale for life. For those who genuinely love their work, and are employed in something beneficial to society, this may not be a problem, but for many work is unpleasant, with little intrinsic value. Sadly, the result of all this work is the degradation of the planet and the creation of an increasingly superfi-cial and mindless culture. The grim 'joke' above the gates of Ausch-witz, 'Work will set you free', has become the mantra of America. The multi-billion dollar pharmaceutical industry tirelessly researches and markets drugs to help us 'work hard and play hard', drugs that numb the pain of both the body and mind.

The persona that must be worn is one of efficiency, hard work, stability, and glowing health. The necessity of melancholy – the nights of the soul – for the creative imagination finds no place. The persona of America glows with rude health, while the real thing pigs out, watches television (mostly advertising in America) and reaches for a painkiller. The image of the individual seems to be increasingly divorced from the psychic reality of actual people. Complex and multifaceted individuals give way to consumers who, cut off from their creative minds, turn to products through which to define themselves. The light and shade of human experience is replaced by virtual experience. Many of our emotions with any real depth are regarded as symptoms needing treatment, and rapture has been replaced by excitement, bliss by strident happiness. Society glorifies production and consumption.

The health of the individual cannot be separated from that of the society in which he or she lives. This is something recognized by most traditional cultures including Renaissance Europe, as testified to by the words of the sixteenth-century physician, Paracelsus:

> If the physician understands things exactly and sees and recognizes all illnesses in the macrocosm outside man, and if he has a clear idea of man and his whole nature, then and only then is he a physician.

> ('The Foundations of Medicine', Paracelsus)

Although there is a growing awareness in society at large of the effects of environment on health and well-being, there seems to be little consideration of the effects of the Zeitgeist on the individual. When the spirit of the age is predatory and exploitive, when people's worth is gauged by their productivity, the human spirit is impoverished and weakened.

Meditation should be like the good physician, but what is understood as meditation is often not meditation at all, from a Buddhist perspective. The concern of Buddhist meditation is to understand the complexity of human life, not to reduce that life to symptoms to be eradicated. What passes as meditation is often simply a relaxation technique. Though this might be useful, it does not attempt to address the whole person. The individual cannot be divorced from the society in which he or she lives or indeed from the macrocosm of all life. In the final analysis, Buddhist meditation is concerned with bringing the individual into a harmonic relationship with reality rather than with the adaptation of the social persona. The purpose of meditation is for the meditator to see the true nature of reality and to live at ease with that reality, the underlying assumption being that true human nature is not different or separate from the rest of reality. If we experience this, we come into a sense of well-being and connectedness that is free of the fear that drives so much human activity. This is not some esoteric, metaphysical doctrine but a pragmatic openness to how things really are. Through meditation we can have an actual experience of the correspondence between ourselves and the rest of life. The reason we so often feel cut off from one another is that we experience the world from a basis of fear and selfishness. Meditation can help us move beyond this egocentric view of the world to one in which we have a sense of place and purpose.

Facing Up to Suffering

Stress implies that we are living under tension, being bent out of shape. We are living in a manner that is distorting us. It is this basic distortion of the human being that Buddhism addresses, not the symptoms it produces. I am not suggesting some Rousseauist idealism that views man as noble but corrupted by an ignoble society. Man has created the society in which he lives and the characteristics of human culture are also inherent in the individual, but just because they are inherent does not mean they are inevitable. Human history testifies not only to the crippling effects of social conditioning, but also to the possibility of overcoming or rising above our given lot. What Buddhism is interested in is our potential to transcend our limitations, traditionally named as the three dominant forces of greed, hatred, and delusion – the third being based in a blinkered understanding of reality. The reduction of stress is only tangential to the realization of this potential.

Buddhism begins with the fact of *dukkha*, which is usually translated 'suffering'. It begins at this point because suffering, in its many varieties, is a universal human experience. No life is free from suffering – stress being a common form. According to Buddhism, when we suffer a possibility opens up, a crack appears in the habitual pattern of our lives. As with all opportunities, we then have a choice – we either enter our experience or do what we can to avoid it.

Meditation is a means by which we can enter more fully into our experience and, by doing so, deepen our understanding of it, and eventually move through it. When meditation is used just as a relaxation, to reduce suffering by avoiding it, it becomes a kind of spiritual aspirin taken to relieve the symptoms, rather than facing up to the deep-rooted patterns that lead to stress and unhappiness.

The positive side of using meditation as a means of combating stress is that our initial limited aims can lead us somewhere unexpected. We start off just wanting to get our shoulders down from around our ears and end up discovering that we are on a spiritual journey. People are sometimes so stressed that they need to reduce the stress to a manageable level before they can consider any journey at all. The danger of using meditation in this way is that we never see beyond the limited benefits of relaxation and use it as a means of sustaining a life that is in desperate need of change. We need to realize that it is not that there is something wrong with our life. This is often the fantasy that we have: that the suffering we experience is somehow unique to us, that the rest of the world is having a jolly good time and it is we who are alone, stressed and at our wit's end. The nature of suffering is that it inclines us towards this kind of near-sighted view of the world. We know that others also suffer — but our emotional reality is one of isolation and negative self-absorption.

One of the most moving stories in the life of the Buddha relates how he helped a woman who had lost her young child.

◆ ◆ ◆

A YOUNG WOMAN, distraught and frantic, is unable to relinquish her dead child. She goes desperately from one person to the next, clasping the corpse to her breast, begging them to heal her baby. One of the people she approaches suggests she goes to see the Buddha, who is staying in the vihara nearby. So the woman hastens to find the Buddha and implores him to cure her child. The Buddha replies that he can indeed help the woman, but that in order to do so he requires a mustard seed, commonly found in all Indian homes. But the Buddha makes one stipulation: the seed must be come from a house where no one has died.

The woman goes off to find the seed, still clutching her dead child. She goes from house to house. Everyone is willing to part with a mustard seed, but no house has been free from the sorrow of death. Again and again, at house after house, she asks. How long the woman searches for the untainted seed we do not know, but at some point her grief takes on a different form. It is transformed into a grief shot through with universal compassion.

In the end she returns to the Buddha, and at last laying down the corpse of her child, asks the Buddha to become her teacher.[11]

◆◆◆

The story shows us the creative power of suffering, from which can arise a greater feeling for life, a sense of compassion that allows us to carry on with a new sensitivity and insight into the human condition. It must be made clear that Buddhism does not court or encourage suffering. On the contrary, Buddhism promotes joy and contentment. But it also recognizes that suffering is unavoidable, deep in the grain of our lives. What is avoidable is the desperate clinging to a fantasy view of what life should be like. Understanding and compassion are capable of transforming our experience from a desperate, frantic state of denial to a state of creative endeavour.

A friend of mine recently lost a child at birth. It was a particularly tragic loss because the pregnancy had followed a previous one that had been extremely difficult, with twins born at the start of the third trimester and at great risk. The twins survived. It had been a great joy for her to have a normal pregnancy after nearly losing both her own life and that of her twins. Sometime after the stillbirth, we held a small memorial service at her home, along with the doctor and midwife and a few friends. People spoke, read poems, and said prayers. Finally, the bereaved mother read something she had written about the death of her child. As she read, sitting with my eyes closed I felt a great release of energy sweep through my body that I can only call bliss. For a while I was quite disconcerted by this, as it seemed an inappropriate response, but I now realize that what I experienced was an opening up to the suffering of the parents, and the experience allowed me to respond more deeply to the grief they felt. It was, I think, a response of compassion, of which I had become more capable because of my willingness to experience my own suffering and impermanence. Although I have not been able to maintain that level of openness, it serves as a reminder of why I practise and why I try to cultivate loving-kindness through the Metta Bhavana meditation. It reminds me that a creative response is possible even when confronted with despair and sadness.

Real Compassion

It is important to recognize that we cannot fix all the pain and suffering in our own lives, let alone the lives of others. We can't make everything better. But there is an alternative to both avoidance and despondency. We can value and deepen our own experience and arrive at a place of real compassion towards ourselves and others. Within compassion there is the possibility of creative action. This requires a type of positive realism. Death, illness, problems in relationships, and all the other frustrations of our lives, are not just going to dissolve in bliss because we meditate. This is the Buddhist version of the American dream. Life is not like that and we know it, yet we still buy in. The truth is that a meaningful, creative life is something for which we must work, something that arises from real effort directed towards noble ends. Such a life is open to all who choose it. We do not have to be particularly clever or talented or good-looking, but we do need to make a consistent effort and be prepared to look honestly at ourselves and the world we are creating. We need to address the needs of our soul, to find a way to access what is deepest in us. We need to follow, not so much our dreams, but our reality. Such a life may be simple with no external great achievements. We will probably never win the Nobel Peace Prize, but we can develop kind- ness and awareness. That is within reach of us all and is a life well lived.

The highest Buddhist ideal is symbolized in the archetypal figures known as Bodhisattvas, beings who have vowed to work tirelessly, through countless lives, for the good of all. Two such figures are the Bodhisattvas known as Avalokita and Tara, who both represent perfect compassion. This is one of the many legends associated with the birth of Tara:

◆ ◆ ◆

AFTER TAKING a vow to end the suffering of all beings, Avalokita worked tirelessly for an unimaginably long time. One day he looked down on the world and saw people suffering in all conceivable ways – through warfare, famine, disease, and bereavement. He was overwhelmed. Despite all his efforts nothing seemed to have changed. Suffering still seemed to be at every door. He began to weep. His tears flowed in a great river. They were so plentiful that a puddle began to form, then a pool, and eventually a vast lake of crystal clear brilliance. Then there arose from the centre of the lake a wondrous lotus, and seated on the lotus was a radiant young woman, green in colour. His tears had brought into being Green Tara, the Bodhisattva of active compassion, serene and playful, full of joy and limitless energy.

◆ ◆ ◆

The spiritual life begins in the facing of suffering, not just the abstract suffering of others but the pain of our own lives. As long as we cling to the fiction of a meaningful life through consumption we numb ourselves to the *dukkha* of our lives. It is ironic that the principal spiritual practice of Buddhism has been co-opted by many into the arsenal of techniques and drugs supposed to make life bearable, but that in the long term they undermine the awareness needed to make changes in the way we live. Meditation is not a way of avoiding this suffering, but a means of cultivating a compassionate and aware response to it.

reflection: Constant Change

Start with the first stage of the Metta Bhavana meditation, that is, cultivating a sense of wishing yourself well. Then reflect that this sense of kindness is not directed towards an idealized you, but you as you actually are.

Bear in mind that in future you are bound to encounter suffering, your own and others', and that there will be disappointments and hardships. Be aware that there is much in your own life that you cannot control, no way that you can insure yourself against the universal truths of old age, sickness, and death. Try to have a sense that these are natural aspects of life – your life, human life, all life.

Be aware that you cannot change reality in regard to the impermanent nature of things and that for kindness to be meaningful it must exist in relation to this reality, not in opposition to it. Don't try to force this reflection but see if there is a way you can open to this impermanence with a sense of kindness and well-wishing towards all life. Try to cultivate a sense that the vitality and beauty of life is dependent on the fact of constant change, as is the suffering. If there is a sense of sadness see if you can sit calmly with it rather than pull away.

Feel the breath in your body and feel that your body is in a constant state of dynamic interaction with the ever-changing world. Try to sit with the breath and the feeling that reflecting in this way evokes a sense of kind understanding, one that is broad enough to engage with the way things really are and not just trying to make everything all right.

Encourage a sense that while life is sad and painful some of the time, life itself could not exist without pain. Use the breath to feel a sense of the fluid nature of your existence, being aware that without this constant taking in and letting out of the breath there would be no life.

As you breathe out try to have a sense of letting go of everything fixed and rigid. Let go into the constantly changing world. Sit for a while with your breath, feeling it bring life into your body as you breathe in and having a sense of letting go into life as you breathe out. Allow your breath to encourage a sense of the movement that is life, being aware of the movement in your body and the movement that is the world outside you. Breathe and have a sense of your place within all this movement that we call life and death.

eight

THE FISH

I caught a tremendous fish
and held him beside the boat
half out of water, with my hook
fast in the corner of his mouth.
He didn't fight.
He hadn't fought at all.
He hung a grunting weight,
battered and venerable
and homely. Here and there
his brown skin hung in strips
like ancient wallpaper,
and its pattern of darker brown
was like wallpaper:
shapes like full-blown roses
stained and lost through age.
He was speckled with barnacles,
fine rosettes of lime,

and infested
with tiny white sea-lice,
and underneath two or three
rags of green weed hung down.
While his gills were breathing in
the terrible oxygen
— the frightening gills,
fresh and crisp with blood,
that can cut so badly —
I thought of the coarse white flesh
packed in like feathers,
the big bones and the little bones,
the dramatic reds and blacks
of his shiny entrails,
and the pink swim-bladder
like a big peony.
I looked into his eyes
which where far larger than mine
but shallower, and yellowed,
the irises backed and packed
with tarnished tinfoil
seen through the lenses
of old scratched isinglass.
They shifted a little, but not
to return my stare.
— It was more like the tipping
of an object toward the light.
I admired his sullen face,
the mechanism of his jaw,
and then I saw

that from his lower lip
— if you could call it a lip —
grim, wet, and weaponlike,
hung five old pieces of fish-line,
or four and a wire leader
with the swivel still attached,
with all their five big hooks
grown firmly in his mouth.
A green line, frayed at the end
where he broke it, two heavier lines,
and a fine black thread
still crimped from the strain and snap
when it broke and he got away.
Like medals with their ribbons
frayed and wavering,
a five-haired beard of wisdom
trailing from his aching jaw.
I stared and stared
and victory filled up
the little rented boat,
from the pool of bilge
where oil had spread a rainbow
around the rusted engine
to the bailer rusted orange,
the sun-cracked thwarts,
the oarlocks on their strings,
the gunnels — until everything
was rainbow, rainbow, rainbow!
And I let the fish go.
  'The Fish', Elizabeth Bishop

When I was about twelve, my friend Andrew and I went fishing. We rode our bikes to a place called Spring Ponds on the outskirts of North London. It was the first time we had been fishing, and we had borrowed rods and other gear from my older brother. Neither of us knew the first thing about the sport and it was to our great surprise that Andy got a bite shortly after casting. What followed was a somewhat traumatic experience. The fish was small, about eight inches long. I think it was a perch. It had swallowed the hook, which we had no idea how to remove. I cannot remember our reasoning, but we decided that we had no option but to kill it. This we tried to do by taking turns at bashing it with a rock. It proved extremely difficult to kill the poor creature, but eventually it lay on the ground bloody and dead. This ended our day's fishing and left us feeling upset and ashamed.

Although I tried fishing a few more times, I always dreaded the idea that I might hook one and have to deal with it. I am glad to say I never did catch another fish. Maybe this childhood incident explains in part why it was that I had such a strong response to Bishop's poem when I first came across it many years later. Perhaps I felt some vicarious redemption for my actions. In the poem, Bishop tells of a fish that fares rather better than our little perch. The poem has become a firm favourite and has led me to explore her poetry further.

This poem, then, is one I often come back to. I regard it as an old friend. I recently used it in a workshop in which we were exploring the imagination in relation to spiritual practice. I was quite surprised that others in the group had quite different views of the poem. Of course I should not have been surprised at this, but I was, for I felt I already knew the poem inside out.

It is in the nature of good poetry always to be open to some degree. A few years ago I had the opportunity to meet one of my favourite poets, Miroslav Holub. I had used one of his poems, 'The Door', in a book I had written, and I brought along a copy of the book thinking to give it to him. During the intermission I had a chance to speak to him and offered him the book, explaining my use of his poem. He refused the book saying that he had already received a copy from the publisher. He then looked directly at me and in his thick, rather gruff Eastern European accent he said, 'The use of my poem was entirely ...' here he paused for a moment and I thought I was going to be rebuked by one of my poetic heroes '... appropriate.'

He went on to explain that he had written the poem about political oppression in his native Czechoslovakia, and that although the use I had put it to was quite different he was happy that I had found another meaning in it. This, then, is one of the characteristics of poetry, that its meaning is not easily exhausted. Poetry has the power it does because when we read it we engage creatively with our imagination. The intention of the poet does not circumscribe the meaning of the poem. While it may be a valid exercise to ask the poet what they meant when they wrote it, we are not, nor should we feel, obliged to limit ourselves to their intended meaning.

One of the reasons Bishop's poem has become dear to me is that I feel it has something important to say about the relationship between compassion and awareness, and the role of the imagination in bringing these two essential qualities together. I have no idea if Bishop had anything of this sort in mind when she wrote the poem, but I trust that she, like Holub, would be happy that I have found meaning and illumination in it.

Beyond Labels

I want to talk a little about 'The Fish' and draw out some of the richness I have found in this wonderful poem. If you are not familiar with Bishop's work I hope you will read it a few times and start to find your own resonance with it before reading on. What follows are a few ideas and feelings that the poem has evoked in me.

We are not told anything about the person who is fishing, or how she comes to find herself in a small boat. We do not know if she is fishing for sport or for food, on a lake or at sea, but by the end of the poem we feel we know a great deal about her, because we have shared with her a genuine human experience. We are never told what type of fish has been caught. That the fish is not named as a carp or a bass seems both unusual and significant. Fishermen will always tell you what sort of fish they have caught; the poem leaves it open. By so doing, the fish is not brought into the human world of science. It is not categorized. It remains in the poetic realm.

There are great advantages in categorizing the world around us from a scientific point of view. It gives us a sense of understanding and security. But it is not always a help to us – as our interest often stops with the establishment of a given category. Once we have established that a tree is an oak, for example, we feel we have no further need to investigate. We think we know what an oak is. 'He is black,' 'She is a mother.' Through naming we know all there is to know and we can order the world and our relationship to it. So in the poem we are not told what type of fish has been hooked, for this is not a type of fish but a very particular fish. We are not able to generalize the individuality of the fish to a species. Rather, we are asked to view this fish as it really is, in all its uniqueness. It is a tremendous fish, not to be categorized. We are being told something very pertinent to an understanding of awareness. Awareness sees everything as unique. Awareness brings an understanding that even the most common sight is never to be repeated and that to see something as it really is we must be free from the habitual tendency to label and categorize. Only then can we truly recognize things for what they are.

This tendency to describe and explain the world with labels is not just restricted to the world outside, but it is often present in our response to our own experience. This is true even for those who are consciously trying to cultivate awareness. When talking to people about their meditation I have often been struck by the superficiality of their interest in their own mental states. They say something like, 'When I meditate I find myself getting angry,' but if you ask them to explain further they are at a loss. They cannot tell you what it feels like to be angry, or what kind of thoughts are associated with the anger. This seems to be true not just for feelings like anger, where it is not difficult to see why there might be a reluctance to investigate further, but for the whole range of distractions that arise when we try to meditate.

When we meditate, we can only be aware of the experience we are actually having. People often seem to think of awareness as something separate from the experience they are having at the time — as if awareness existed independently of their moment to moment experience. It is quite easy to be aware if we feel calm and happy, but the real challenge of meditation is to learn how we can bring awareness to the whole range of mental states that we inhabit. This sometimes means we have to go rather deeper than just giving them a label like anger, and really try to get a sense of what they are like. I am not suggesting here a psychoanalytical approach to our experience, but a sense of how we can just be with our experience more fully. The attempt to 'understand' or analyse our experience often takes us away from the experience itself into rationalization and the safety of the dominant intellect. Just as if when we are with a friend, and we are constantly trying to figure out what they really mean rather than just attending to them, we lose sight of the friend entirely and become lost in our own small world.

Responding to What is There

Back in the world of the poem, we get a very detailed description of the fish – not only its appearance, but also some sense of its history. We learn that it has had many encounters with humans, and repeatedly escaped capture. Through sustained observation we enter into a relationship with it. What gives the poem some of its strength is that the fish is not anthropomorphized, as animals so often are. It remains a fish. The eyes of the fish hold no awareness. They do not return the stare 'more like the tipping of an object towards the light'. We are not asked to believe the fish is anything more than a fish. Our relationship to the fish does not depend on the attribution of qualities it does not really possess. This, too, is important, for the nature of compassion is a response to what is actually there; it is not based in some romantic or sentimental idea.

Compassion is not the projection of our needs and desires on to a person or situation outside ourselves. The basis of compassion is loving-kindness. It is loving-kindness that we try to develop through the practice of the Metta Bhavana meditation. Compassion arises when loving-kindness, or metta, comes into contact with suffering. It is the desire to alleviate suffering. It is said that metta has both a far enemy and a near enemy. The far enemy is its opposite, hatred. Its near enemy looks a lot like metta itself. This near enemy is known as *pema*, which has been translated as 'sticky affection', a kind of sentimentality. This kind of sentimentality is often exploited, albeit for good ends. Pandas and tigers are the poster children of the wildlife campaigns. You never see 'Save the Scorpion'. Pema is the attribution of feelings to something, or someone, that are essentially self-referential. They do not have a real basis in the situation, but are our own feelings projected on to another. It is quite different from real empathy (although much of what gets called empathy is nearer to pema).

Empathy occurs when, through deep appreciation, we are able to feel something of another person's condition. Pema is quite superficial and will break down if the situation conflicts with our own desires and needs. Pema leaves us open to the exploitation of guilt; we give because we are made to feel bad about our relative good fortune. Loving-kindness is a response to a situation that is not based in sentimentality or guilt but is a natural response based in a sense of positive self-love. We see a situation to which we are in a position to respond. Something is needed and we are able to help. We often find it is not easy to respond in this way. This is an important realization, as it indicates a lack of the positive self-regard on which metta and compassion depend. If we are able to see clearly how we are inhibited from responding with kindness and love, we can be inspired to take up a meditation like the Metta Bhavana.

It sometimes strikes people as strange that we should consciously have to develop kindness. It seems rather artificial and forced to deliberately try to cultivate it, but realistically this is the situation that many of us find ourselves in, and it is not going to change unless we are prepared to do something about it.

Here is the real strength of Buddhist meditation practice. It give us the means to effect real change in our emotional patterns and in the ways in which we look at ourselves and the world. It takes a lot of courage to admit to ourselves that we are often unkind and selfish. But such self-awareness also opens up great possibilities for change. Perhaps most fundamentally we need to have faith that we can change, that we are not forever trapped by our negative states of mind. This is the very foundation of metta, a self-directed kindness that is able to see ourselves as we are, with all our strengths and weaknesses. Once we face ourselves with kindness we will be able to begin to change in the manner that we would like. Furthermore, when we accept ourselves in this way we will find that feeling kindness for others becomes far easier.

For metta to be developed we have to try to see things, not in some romanticized way, but as near as we can to how they actually are. This does not mean that the type of awareness we are trying to develop is cold or detached. Because Buddhism talks quite often about detachment, it is important to realize that it is detachment from greed, hatred, and prejudice that prevents us from responding lovingly and creatively. It does not imply a hard indifference to suffering, either our own or that of those around us.

It is possible, as the poem suggests, to have a real emotional response that is not based in a falsification of the situation. If we look closely and carefully enough, our imagination becomes engaged. Imagination is an emotional quality. When we take the time to really appreciate something, we enter into a relationship with it. We do not have to remake it in our own image. We give it the uniqueness that it really has. We enter into what I would call a poetic relationship, where meaning is heightened from the dull level on which we tend to operate most of the time. The word 'poem' is derived from a Greek word meaning 'to create'. So the poetic act is creative; it is the creation of a relationship, and within that relationship there is a sense of meaning. Through awareness, we come into relationship with the world and with others. Without awareness, we are not even in relationship with ourselves and we are cut off from the world. Whether or not we come into a meaningful relationship with ourselves and with others is, in the end, a matter of choice. We cannot just decide to do it and therefore it happens; it is a choice, in the sense that we can choose to foster and encourage a wish to do so as one of the primary intentions of our lives.

To live life more poetically does not mean walking around with our head in the clouds, but to walk with our feet firmly on the ground and to have a real feeling of connection with the world and with other people. It requires taking the time, and making the effort, to strengthen these connections.

A Ritual Approach to Life

To live more in relationship implies there is a shift from a self-centred and self-referential position to one that is increasingly aware of the interdependent nature of life. We often find that this type of awareness is encouraged and strengthened through adopting what we might term a more ritualistic approach to life. Ritual, in this sense, is a means of bringing a heightened awareness to our activity. In Tibetan Buddhism, which is very rich in ritual, one is encouraged to treat whatever object is being employed in ritual as representing ultimate reality. Flowers, for example, are regarded as being imbued with significance; their beauty and fragility reflect the true nature of all reality, which is impermanent and subject to decay, just like our own bodies. Thus we imagine that the flowers we are offering are imbued with a meaning that goes beyond words.

This, then, is the opposite of the habitual way in which we approach much of the activity that makes up our lives. Take, for example, the making and drinking of a cup of tea. This can mean throwing a tea bag in a cup of hot water and drinking it while we watch television, or the highly refined and aware activity that makes up the Japanese tea ceremony. In such a ritual we give ourselves over completely to the tea. Everyday habitual activity becomes a metaphor for the whole of life. We are in a real and imaginative relationship with the fundamental elements of life: the element of fire that we use to heat the water, the water itself, and its interaction with the organic world.

Whatever we do – we can choose to do it in such a manner that the richness of the activity is brought more intensely into awareness. When we bring ourselves more fully to an activity, that activity takes on a sense of meaning that it does not have otherwise. By creating a little space at the beginning and end of things, life is less of a continuous frenzy of activity. We are not trying to experience the world in a false way, but trying to realize that our normally unmindful attitude to life robs us of the depth and meaning that is there all the time.

In the poem, the fish is seen as it really is. It is hard not to be moved by the care and attention with which it is described. The fish is made vivid for us, brought to life. It is described as a complete universe in itself, a home for barnacles and tiny white sea lice. We understand that this fish is part of a different world, not our own; part of an intricate interdependent world from which it has been removed and brought into the terrible oxygen of our own. There is no suggestion that this fish feels like we would if we were suddenly snatched from all that is familiar and sustaining. The fish hangs like a grunting weight.

Transformation of Awareness

There is a certain ambiguity in the conclusion to the poem. What is clear is that the fish is 'seen' and then released back into its own world. Victory fills the small boat. Is this simply the victory of catching the fish? I choose to understand this rather differently. It seems to me that the victory is that of both the fish and the fisher. The fish regains its freedom. Something extraordinary takes place; all becomes 'rainbow, rainbow, rainbow!' The beauty of poetry is partly that its meaning is not static or fixed. We are free to take what we wish. For me there is something in the detail and beauty of the description of the fish that implies a relationship established between the poet and the fish. It is of course, a one-sided relationship. The fish remains a fish, but the poet experiences the fish with a heightened awareness. The real victory is the transformation of awareness, a coming into relationship with the world in a deeper way. Once the fish has been seen in this way it has to be returned to the water, as it becomes more than an object of sport or source of food.

We are able to treat ourselves and others with callous indifference only because we choose to have a partial and alienated view of them. Hatred and acts of hatred show a lack of imagination. We are able to see the world only in terms of our limited needs and desires. We are unable to imagine the humanity of those at whom the hatred is directed. There is a story of three people; a builder, a scientist, and a poet, looking at a tree. The first sees the tree and thinks, 'I could build a whole house from all that wood.' The scientist sees the tree and thinks about its structure, how it grew, and its relationship to the environment, while the poet sees the tree and is struck by its beauty, and their awareness becomes heightened. The poet becomes elevated by its beauty and life.

This is a story that is now being played out in many parts of the world. In northern California a great fight has been mounted to save what few old-growth redwoods remain. Coastal redwoods require very particular conditions. They grow slowly over hundreds of years. In these magnificent trees, some of which are 2,000 years old, protesters have found a powerful symbol that speaks against the avarice and short-sightedness that characterizes much of our relationship to the world. For others, the trees are a means of livelihood and have no value besides that of the timber they produce. Of course, if you are a logger and the welfare of your family depends on your being able to work, it is understandable that you might feel that the value of such trees is commercial. It is all too easy to condemn others when we live in comfort.

The point I wish to make is more that we can look at the world in different ways. We can see it in a utilitarian manner where it exists purely for our benefit, we can see it as a fascinating and complex puzzle that we wish to understand, or we can enter into it poetically and to some degree break down, or at least weaken, the sense of separation between self and other.

It is interesting to think a little about how we relate to the natural world. We very often speak of it as something quite different from the human world. Even the terminology we employ is interesting. We talk about the 'natural world', or about 'nature', as if we are somehow separate from it. But there is nothing in our lives that has not come from the natural world: the houses we live in, the clothes we wear, the food we eat. It is true that much of this is highly processed, but all the raw material has come from nature, from the natural world. As our dominance of the world has grown, so our respect for it has diminished. As we grow more affluent, so we become more and more impoverished. Through losing our relationship with the earth that sustains us, we lose contact with our soul – for there can be no deeper sense of ourselves than that which has a basis in these relationships.

It is not sentimentality or romanticism that should motivate us to care about our world, but an awareness of our interdependence with that world. And there can be no real awareness without imagination. In an age when we can walk into a supermarket and buy whatever food we wish, we need have no direct contact with the production of that food. We are not going to go back to a time when the natural rhythms of the world were also the rhythms of our lives, so we need to use our awareness as a means to develop a deeper sense of, and care for, the environment and all life on the planet.

We cannot separate awareness and compassion. Awareness without compassion is sterile and lacks depth – it reduces others to statistics – while compassion without awareness is blind and unable to respond creatively to real situations. Awareness married to compassion allows a real relationship to develop. It is only through understanding, through a feeling of relationship to the world, that we can go beyond the selfishness that characterizes so much of the modern world. In Buddhism, wisdom is the fruit of this union. Wisdom sees everything as it really is: sees the impermanence of all things, but also the uniqueness of all things – and understands that everything is in relationship with everything else. This is not a wisdom detached from the real world, but a wisdom able to feel the suffering of the world, able to feel the pain that results from our isolation and lack of poetic relationship to the world, and able to respond to that pain and isolation in others. This wisdom is the real victory a human life offers us – 'until everything was rainbow, rainbow, rainbow!'

reflection: Active Listening

The next time a friend begins to tell you something about themselves, see if you can maintain a balanced awareness between you. Pay attention to your breath, using this focus to help you be aware of your responses on the level of sensations in your body, rather than just thoughts.

Try really to take the other person in: look at them, notice their expression and tone of voice. See if you can think a little less and sense a little more. Encourage them to go deeper into what they are saying, giving them your attention while maintaining an awareness of yourself. Try not to finish their sentences in your mind before they do.

See if you can have an open attitude, noticing when you get caught up in your own thoughts and then coming back to your breath and the other person. Be open to the situation: even if you have heard your friend talk about the same thing many times, try to hear them as if for the first time.

Breathe and remind yourself that you do not have to know or understand – all you need do is be attentive and kind. See if you can suspend coming to a premature understanding of the situation and be content just to witness what is happening in you and your friend as you communicate. Don't try to control the situation; just be interested in it as it unfolds.

Don't rush to fill the spaces in a conversation, but use any silence to come back to yourself, being aware of your body and your breath.

Talking in this way does not mean you have to be over-intense; try to let your attention be relaxed but at the same time engaged with what is happening.

This kind of active listening, listening to ourselves in terms of being aware of ourselves and listening to the other person, will encourage both a deeper empathy with our friend and a deeper understanding of ourselves. When we can listen in this way we begin to see more clearly how often we jump to conclusions and how much of what passes for communication is just two people talking at one another rather than talking together. Of course, there is also a place for light social conversation, so use your common sense.

reflection: Everyday Ritual

Take an everyday activity, such as a household task of which you are not very fond, and approach it in a different way. Whenever we have to do a task that we don't enjoy, we usually try to get it over as quickly as possible. We want to get it out of the way so that we can do something we enjoy. So the first thing we need to do is give ourselves enough time to do the job well.

Take cleaning the bathroom, for example. If you think you can rush through it in ten minutes, decide to give yourself half an hour. Before you begin, sit down for a few minutes and think how you feel about having to clean the bathroom. Then resolve to do it well, even though you acknowledge that you have a resistance. Reflection can help. You might reflect that the bathroom is a place where you attend to the basic needs of your body, that keeping clean is an act of respect towards yourself and others. Spiritual purification is often marked by a ritual washing of some kind. It's a useful and worthwhile task. One of the tasks that Hercules was given was the cleaning of the Augean stables. It is interesting that this task, though immense, was essentially menial. This might all sound a bit bizarre, but that's fine – you can have a bit of a sense of humour about it as well.

Next, consider what you need to do the job well and how you are going to set about it. Before you actually start, be clear in your mind what you are going to do. See if you can think of some extra little touch that will improve the quality of the bathroom. Most importantly, encourage yourself to attend to the task as fully as possible. Do it with an attitude of attention and care. Be aware how you are using your body, and stop every now and then to become aware of your breath. When you have finished sit down again for a few minutes, and be aware how you feel having completed the task well.

reflection: Interconnections

Sit down in meditation posture, taking time to become aware of your body and its sensations. Use an awareness of your breath to develop a sense of calm and clarity. Once you feel settled just bring to mind your normal morning routine. Think about what you do when you get out of bed, and then reflect on all that has happened to allow you to act as you do.

Think of the clothes you are wearing, and the people that work in the stores where you bought them, those involved in the transportation of those clothes from perhaps thousands of miles away, the people who worked to make them, those who grew the cotton or tended the sheep to produce the raw materials. Have a sense of all the labour that went into what you wear, an extensive network, perhaps spanning the globe.

Do the same with the food you eat, but together with all the human labour have a sense also of the natural world: the basic elements of warmth and light, the rain, the earth, without which the production of food would be impossible.

Recollect that everything in your world is of the world; that everything that fills our life has come from elements that have existed, in one form or another, since the beginning of the universe; that all that exists now, even those things that seem most permanent, will exist in a different form in the future.

Be aware that this is also true in relation to your body; that it too is made up of a fantastic combination of the elements that make up the universe. Reflect for a moment on yourself as a particular manifestation of energy, matter, and mind – an open system that is in constant interchange with other systems, constantly dependent on the air you breathe, the food you eat, constantly manifesting, never discrete or independent from the rest of life. Let the mind be open in this way, not so much thinking, but allowing, your mind to be in a state of open wonder.

Then come back to the breath: this ever-present experience of breathing in and out. Let the mind settle back on the breath, then sit for a few minutes without doing anything at all. Just sit.

nine

ROMANCING DEATH

Whenever you see the hearse go by
And think to yourself you're gonna die,
Be merry, my friends, be merry.

They put you in a big white shirt
And cover you over with tons of dirt,
Be merry, my friends, be merry.

They put you in a long-shaped box
And cover you over with tons of rocks,
Be merry, my friends, be merry.

The worms crawl out and the worms crawl in,
The ones that crawl in are lean and thin,
The ones that crawl out are fat and stout,
Be merry, my friends, be merry.

Your eyes fall in and your hair falls out
And your brains come tumbling down your snout,
Be merry, my friends, be merry.

'Be Merry', Anon

My interest in poetry began not with whole poems, but with their titles and first lines. Having been brought up without poetry, I was tentative and suspicious of it. This began to change when my older brother stole a copy of Dylan Thomas's *Collected Poems* from our school library. What it was doing there I don't know, as my school seemed as suspicious of poetry as I was. It had a wonderfully seductive dust-jacket; Thomas, cigarette in mouth, pen in hand, artfully haggard. He seemed so sexy, and some of his first lines are really very fine. (I still love reading the first line index in poetry books – Sylvia Plath is my favourite, she has some wonderful first lines.) Slowly I moved on from first lines and began to read and re-read some of the more accessible of Thomas's poems. Although it seems very obvious to me now, when I was an adolescent I had no idea that you might read something more than once for pleasure. You read something and that was it. The greatest failure of my dismal education was that no effort was made to encourage any appreciation of literature.

The only poem I can remember from school was that read by the deputy headmaster, a small Welshman with a naval bearing, every time he was required to lead the morning assembly. It was, I think, by Kipling and concerned putting away the diversions of childhood and taking up the responsibilities of manhood. It was claustrophobically Victorian, its message alien and repressive to adolescent boys whose voices were breaking and whose bodies were erupting – even though Mr Jones did have a strong Welsh voice and read it rather well. Any reading we were required to do felt like a forced march with full pack. Reading aloud was a form of mild torture which laid you bare to the sarcasm of both teacher and classmates. The idea of repeatedly reading the same thing would have reminded us of one of Dante's inner hells — if we'd had any idea of who Dante was. Nevertheless, the music of Thomas, and his dark eroticism, brought me back to him again and again. I was struck by what I would now call the moistness of his words, words that seemed to have been grown in the shade, in dark wet woods. And it seemed that death lurked between many of the lines.

In Touch with Death

Years later, as a volunteer at a Zen hospice, I would find myself recalling one of Thomas's poems, 'Do not go gently into that good night.' It seemed a valid point of view, and somehow captured the uneasy feeling I had about the value we at the hospice put on a 'good death'. This is one of many occasions on which I've felt that a poem or story that made an early impression on me has given weight to a vague, uneasy feeling — a feeling given its meaning by an association with something that has become part of my memory, and therefore part of my experience. This feeling came from my inability to be as human as I would have liked when confronted with death. The problem for me was finding common ground. I now realize that the common ground is our shared fear of death and our complete ignorance of death as an experience. Thomas would not have us forget the fearfulness of death. Wittgenstein comments in the Tractatus 'Death is not an event in life: death is not lived through.' While Buddhists may disagree with Wittgenstein, believing that in some sense there is a continuity of consciousness after death, he neverthe-less hits a nerve for me. Certainly we do not experience our own death in the normal sense of human experience. It seems to me that such an unknowing is the core of what has become known as existential anxiety, and that our choice is either to try to avoid such anxiety or to face up to it.

I find little comfort in the back-from-the-dead-blissful-golden-light reports from people who have been clinically 'dead' for a matter of seconds. One fear I have is that death lasts for a long time, a couple of seconds of bliss fails to reassure me. I have had plenty of life experiences that start off with a little bliss, but that is only the start. One aspect of the New Age phenomenon is a revival of the redemptive death, the idea that a life can be redeemed by a noble death. This is only a short step away from the death-bed conversions available to anyone who will accept them. I am reminded of the rumour that Frank Sinatra, when seriously ill, offered a large sum for the Pope to hear his confession.

I was once asked to lead some meditation on a day event for volunteers at the Zen hospice project. I had stopped volunteering some years previously, but I retain an admiration for both the organization and its volunteers. I spoke about two things in particular: that none of us understand death, and that a good death is no substitute for a good life. It is possible to have a short, tragic life, self-centred and destructive, but to die well. I wonder at this, and I have found it inspiring and moving to witness it, but I do not feel it makes up for life. That would demean life. I will not be too worried if I go raging. I struggle to bring awareness of death into my life, but death is still a stranger to me and I have never been very good with strangers.

Perhaps it is too easy to fool ourselves that we have become familiar with death. Attending to the dying, reflecting on death as a spiritual practice, and experiencing the death of loved ones, it can begin to seem as if we have made our peace with death. But death always remains a stranger. To some extent we can be comfortable with the end of life, but death is not just the end of life, it is the unknowable eternity that awaits. There seem to be some advantages in living in unknowing apprehension of death. The common alternatives of believing in an eternal afterlife or in nothing at all both seem too glib, too easy.

A superficial knowledge of Buddhism suggests that Buddhists believe in rebirth – sometimes incorrectly called reincarnation. Reincarnation is a misunderstanding of the Buddha's teaching, as it implies that something like a soul is reborn in another body. But Buddhism is very clear in denying that there is a soul – in the sense of some kind of enduring and unchanging entity – or anything else, that is available to be reincarnated.

Buddhism avoids the two extremes of complete annihilation and eternal life. This position is an uncomfortable one, as it leaves us without a simple, certain explanation. The idea of some kind of volitional process continuing after death – which cannot be identified simply with the dead person but neither can it be seen as completely independent from them – is quite a difficult one. As with so much of the Buddha's teaching, the intention seems to be not to present us with pat answers but to point us in the direction of deeper thought and contemplation.

The Urgency of Life

Buddhism emphasizes death in order to bring the urgency of life more vividly into focus. Whenever we seriously consider death we are brought to the point of asking questions, not only about death itself, but about the meaning of life in the face of the fact of death. The Tibetan tradition teaches the possibility of gaining liberation at the time of death and places importance on the quality of consciousness at the moment of death. This does not mean that the volition of a whole lifetime, or many lifetimes, can be easily turned around at this point. It is perhaps an opportunity that we might do well to prepare for, but it is not an easy one to seize.

During one of our meditation days, I heard the following story which dramatically illustrates this point.

◆ ◆ ◆

A WESTERN DISCIPLE was on a retreat, led by a well-known teacher, in South-east Asia. At some point the retreat was interrupted by a local villager asking the teacher to attend a dying man and instruct him in the Dharma. The teacher said he was unable to come but would ensure the man got a Buddhist funeral. There were a number of Americans on the retreat, and one in particular was outraged at the seeming lack of compassion shown by the teacher. Summoning his courage he confronted the teacher.

The teacher was quite old and used a stick. Evidently he was still quite vigorous, for his response to the American was to pin him to the ground with his walking stick pressed against his throat. The teacher then started to instruct him in the Dharma. The poor man, in such a situation, was completely unable to understand what the teacher was telling him. The other students understood the point the teacher was making: if one has not attended to one's spiritual welfare during life, it is too late to expect to understand the Dharma in the confusion and fear of death – far greater confusion than that caused by an old man pressing a walking stick to your throat. On the other hand, if one has paid attention to the cultivation of awareness and compassion in one's life, and lived an ethical life, there is no fear of death.

◆ ◆ ◆

We might find such teaching methods extreme (and no doubt in America they would result in a lawsuit) but they clearly had a beneficial effect on the students. For me, the story illustrates the intense commitment of the teacher in trying to communicate the importance of consistent practice while one has the opportunity. He did not want his students to find themselves in the position of the villager, and he was able to put the unfortunate man's death to good use by impressing on the students the urgency of practice.

The truth is that none of us knows when our death will come. For the few that die in the loving and supportive environment of a well-run hospice, there are thousands who die watching television or crossing the road. Death does not wait until we are ready. It comes like a wolf out of a pitch-black night and will take a lamb as readily as an old ewe. For most, there is not even the time, or presence of mind, to rage against it. It is important that we do not fall into some vague, New Age, romanticized idea that somehow death will be a positive and liberating affair. We should perhaps fear death, for we do not know what will follow. This fear of death can help us to make the most of our lives. We should put our mind at rest by living a life about which we feel good, a life that is useful, a life where we strive to manifest what is best in us, for it is in this way that we prepare ourselves for death and overcome our fear.

In the Gap

Perhaps the best known Buddhist text on death is the *Bardo Thödol*, sometimes referred to as the *Tibetan Book of the Dead*. The *Bardo Thödol* gives a detailed description of what happens when we die. It speaks to us not in the language of the rational mind, but through image and symbol. Perhaps because Carl Jung wrote a lengthy commentary to the famous translation by Lama Kazi Dawa-Samdup, it has attracted much attention from those interested in archetypal psychology. It is a fascinating text that presents a picture of the after-death experience with an immense appeal to the intuitive mind. Although it is clear that the Buddhas and other figures that appear in the visionary experience of the 'afterlife' relate to Tibetan cultural and religious beliefs, they also have a depth that goes beyond any particular culture. We find that although the initial experience of death is similar to the common 'white light' experience, this experience is overwhelming, not comforting, and the experience of the bardo soon becomes terrifying and intimidating, so we seek relief from it in rebirth.

Traditionally, the *Bardo Thödol* is read over the corpse of the deceased in order to offer instruction to the consciousness as it traverses the bardo between one life and the next. The primary purpose of the text is to help the hearer gain liberation from rebirth. Failing that, it tries to guide the consciousness towards a favourable rebirth. It is not perhaps too hard to imagine how, if confronted with the pure white light, which appears to symbolize consciousness in its fundamental pure state, we would panic and seek out the more familiar.

On a rather more mundane level, we have these bardo experiences quite often. We find ourselves in situations that have a little too much reality for our liking and we find ways of distracting ourselves from those experiences. Indeed, for many people it is very hard just to sit still in meditation. The mind is troubled and distracted, we find we are not able to stay with the simple situation of just being with our breath, or just being aware of our emotions on a deeper level. It is rather unrealistic, then, to think that when we die, and find ourselves separated from our body, separated from the ones we love, separated from all that is familiar to us, that we will be able to keep ourselves together. To be able to make use of such an extreme situation would require us to have developed a very stable and emotionally positive awareness. Such an awareness takes a great deal of effort and practice. The point of the teachings we find in the *Bardo Thödol* is to impress upon us the urgency of making good use of our human form while we are able to do so.

Life and Death

Death, particularly the death of those close to us, can be used to great benefit. No one dies in vain if those close to them are prepared to try to understand the teaching that death offers. I was very inspired by a close friend with whom I lived. His father died after being seriously ill for many years, but he had faced life with cheerfulness and an inner vitality undiminished by his long fight with cancer. When death came, he was at peace with his life. His son had made sure he spent time with him during the last few years, even though they were living on different continents. When his father died, my friend took the time he needed to really absorb the death. He was profoundly affected by it, but was able to be fully with the emotions that he felt. Sometimes this meant staying with painful and powerful mental states. His ability to do this was largely due to his having meditated for many years. The effect of his father's death was an obvious deepening of his character, and a vigorous resolve to use his own life positively and creatively. This process of absorption and integration took many months and is, I am sure, still going on. It was a wonderful example to me of the positive power of death for those left behind.

Death provides us with an opportunity to look more closely at life, but it is not an easy opportunity to take. If we are not used to staying with our emotions, it is very hard to be with death. We tend to see it as an enemy, as the opposite of life, but it is clear that life and death are not two opposing forces but simply two aspects of one force. Here is another well-known Dylan Thomas poem:

> The force that through the green fuse drives the flower
> Drives my green age; that blasts the roots of trees
> Is my destroyer.
> And I am dumb to tell the crooked rose
> My youth is bent by the same wintry fever.
>
> The force that drives the water through the rocks
> Drives my red blood; that dries the mouthing streams
> Turns mine to wax.
> And I am dumb to mouth unto my veins
> How at the mountain spring the same mouth sucks.
>
> The hand that whirls the water in the pool
> Stirs the quicksand; that ropes the blowing wind
> Hauls my shroud sail.
> And I am dumb to tell the hanging man
> How of my clay is made the hangman's lime.
>
> The lips of time leech to the fountain head;
> Love drips and gathers, but the fallen blood
> Shall calm her sores.
> And I am dumb to tell a weather's wind
> How time has ticked a heavens round the stars.

And I am dumb to tell the lover's tomb
How at my sheet goes the same crooked worm.

There is an undeniable reality to death that is hard to stay with. I once
saw a very interesting documentary on the preparation of corpses for
viewing in an American mortuary. It was difficult to sit through, and
a number of people walked out. I will not go into detail, but one saw
the very invasive techniques used to make the dead look alive. It was
disturbing to witness the abuse of a dead body in order to shield the
living from the universal truth of death. This in stark contrast to the
simple, dignified, and respectful preparation of the dead I have helped
with in hospice. There we would gently and carefully wash the body
and dress it as the deceased had requested. This would be done by
people who had a real feeling for the dead person and who had cared
for them in life. It was a very moving and positive experience and a
way of expressing a final tenderness towards them. There was no
cutting into the body, no draining of fluids, no intravenous embalming
by technicians who had no connection with the person. Another day,
another dead body. Even the dead have to look good.

Real contact with death is a privilege. It is a great loss that our
society has largely commercialized, sanitized, and sentimentalized
death. It means that we are less able to live fully. Our culture is
increasingly turning its back on the everyday reality of death, choosing
instead to reduce death to entertainment. When death comes it will
be all the more frightening. The acceptance of death as the silent twin
to life, life coming to an end, should not be understood as a hardening
towards life. To be callous towards death is to deny life. In contrast,
it is a sense of tenderness and compassion towards life that makes the
acceptance of death possible. What we can learn from death is that

kindness gives life to our relationships, which cannot then be measured by time.

As we witness a life coming to an end each moment becomes precious. A sense of mortality can give weight to our own lives. As we age we begin to sense how our seemingly sequential experience of life has a depth of past to it. We realize that our lives are played out in a world where the past gives meaning and shape to the present – our own personal past, the past of our culture, and the collective past of human kind. Our experience is organized, patterned, by both our directed experience and the experience inherent in human consciousness. The wisdom of a text like the *Bardo Thödol* lies in its resonance with basic patterns in the human psyche that have a collective reality.

Maturity is rooted in experience that has been aged, held within the vessel of the psyche, gaining flavour and depth. Maturity can bring a sense of empathy with life, for as our experience gains texture we find increasing points of contact with others. The deeper our experience the more we find ourselves occupying the territory that is common to all. One of the strongest bonds with life is a fuller realization that we all die. We all take the same walk into the shadows. Sometimes on a crowded bus or train I find myself looking around at the faces. Some are old, lined with life. Some are still wide-eyed at it all. I know that, at some point, all the people I see will die. Such a reflection may seem depressing, but it also has the potential to bring life into a sharper focus. Such a seeing into the future can evoke a sense of attention and care in us. We will never see this particular collection of faces again. As we return together from work or the shops we are making another journey together through time.

The recollection of death as a universal occurrence interferes with our normal, linear idea of time. This is because we realize that time, at least for us as individuals, is finite, it does not go on and on. When we can hold in mind the finite nature of 'our' time, each moment is heavy with the past, rich and deep with its joys and sadness. Each moment is pregnant with the future. We can have a fuller sense of life, continuously issuing from the present, which is full and fecund with the past.

When we are more aware of death some moments in time can enter into a completely different ocean of time, which we can perhaps call the soul. They are caught in a web of meaning, amplified. They remain with us, their waves moving concentrically outwards, slowly diffusing, giving meaning to our lives. To understand life as an infinite future is to place ourselves in a life which has no history and no meaning. To open ourselves to life requires that we honour its transience and vulnerability, having a sense of the present opening out of the past and towards death.

reflection: Letting Go

Start by spending a little time setting up your posture. Take as much time as you need to become aware on the simple level of your body and its sensations. You can use an awareness of your breath to encourage this sense of your body. Just gently follow your breath as it comes and goes in the body. Let the breath be easy and relaxed; don't try to force anything. Just being with your breath in this way will naturally bring awareness down into your body.

Staying with the breath, have a sense of it having always been with you. From the moment of birth your breath has been your constant companion. Reflect on the breath as you feel it. Have a sense of your breath continuing throughout your life, a thread of experience linking every moment, weaving together the minutes, hours, days, years of your life, in every waking and sleeping moment.

Be aware of your breath as a subtle reflection of your body and feelings, whether fast or slow, easy or laboured, in relation to the different experiences in your life. Reflect that your breath is the most consistent aspect of your life. All through the physical transformation from newborn baby to adult it has been there, the most basic sustaining element of life. Try then to have a sense of welcoming the breath into the your body, opening the body to the breath. Have an awareness of how the body takes what it needs and then lets the breath return to the world.

Have a sense of yourself as a breathing body in a breathing world, a world of people, animals, plants, and trees – all breathing in their own way. Have a feeling of sharing your breath with the world. As you breathe in, be aware that you are breathing the outside world into the world of your own body.

Now bring to mind that one day, at an unknown time in the future, the breath will leave your body and not return. So as you breathe out try to have a sense of letting go of your breath as fully as possible. Let it freely go back to the world it came from. Breathing in, welcome the breath, have a sense of appreciation for it, then let it go again. With each new breath open the body to life, then let it go back to the world of life. Try to have a sense of not taking the breath for granted, but of recognizing its preciousness, and let go of each out-breath as fully as possible, knowing that one day you will have to let go of it completely. Now stop trying to do anything at all, just sit quietly, letting the mind relax, just breathing.

APPENDIX

The Mindfulness of Breathing

Mindfulness is a bright and expansive mental state. Sometimes it is said that a concentrated mind is a happy mind, and this happily concentrated mind is relaxed. It is mindfulness. Mindfulness includes a strong element of interest and pleasure. There is a sense of expansion to it, a sense of opening up rather than narrowing down. At the same time, there is a sense of clarity and purpose. The mind is balanced, poised, and full of creative energy.

The breath is part of us and at the same time something to be directly experienced. It is very simple, but our experience of it can be tremendously fulfilling and rich. It can become a direct experience of life ebbing and flowing within us. This awareness of ourselves is the best foundation for a greater awareness of all that is around us.

The Mindfulness of Breathing is the bedrock of all meditation practice. Other more exotic practices, such as the visualization of archetypal figures that embody spiritual virtues from the Tibetan

---

tradition, are powerful exercises on their own level, but without a firm foundation in basic awareness they are little more than pleasant distractions.

If we really want to make changes in ourselves, we need first to be aware of where we are starting from – what we are now. And this awareness is developed pre-eminently by the practice of mindfulness. All forms of meditation need a strong element of mindfulness or we will simply become distracted. Without mindfulness we might achieve a pleasant enough state of mind, but we cannot really call it meditation.

I love the Mindfulness of Breathing. After many years of regular practice it is still the meditation I enjoy most. It has a simplicity and directness I have not found in any other practice. All we have to do is be aware of our breath. Nothing could be simpler. Yet it is a practice to last a lifetime, becoming richer and richer over the years, and contributing in a very direct way to the rest of our lives. Let's take a look at the structure of the practice itself.

If you were to sit in a good posture and gently bring attention to your breath, bringing the mind back to the breath when it drifted away – you would be practising the Mindfulness of Breathing. It is that simple. But although it is very simple in theory it can be quite difficult in practice, so it is structured in a way that leads us from easier exercises of mindfulness to more challenging ones. It has four distinct stages, which I shall briefly describe. (In my previous book, *Change Your Mind*, I also lead the reader through a guided meditation.)[12]

The meditation should be preceded by some time spent setting up a good posture and becoming aware of the body. To start with, the whole meditation, including the preparation, should be kept fairly short, say fifteen to twenty minutes. Make the four stages roughly the same length.

It is far better to do a short period of meditation that you enjoy than trying to meditate for longer and becoming uncomfortable and distracted, so that your meditation just seems like hard work. More experienced meditators often find that forty to fifty minutes is a good length of time, but this is too long for most beginners. If you enjoy meditation you will find you naturally lengthen your periods of meditation as your body gets used to the posture and you learn to become absorbed more easily.

Once you have settled down a bit and taken in how you are feeling through being aware of your body, bring your attention to the breath. It is important to realize that this meditation is not a breathing exercise; we are not trying to breathe in a 'spiritual' way, or do some kind of yoga exercise. We are just letting our breathing be as natural as possible. If you find that your breath changes, fine – it is a living thing – but don't deliberately alter it; just stay with it.

Stage One

At the end of an out-breath count to yourself 'one'; after the next out-breath count 'two'; after the next, 'three', and so on. Continue counting silently after each out-breath until you reach ten. Then start again at one and repeat as before. In both this stage and the next, remember that you are meant to be mindful not of the counting, not the numbers, but the breath. The counting just helps you to realize when your attention has wandered, which might at first be quite common.

Stage Two

This is different from the first stage only in that you change – or make as if to change – the point at which you count. You still count between each exhalation and the inhalation that follows, but you now count just before the in-breath, so you are anticipating the next breath rather than marking the breath you've already taken. Although you might feel you are counting in the same place, this stage actually feels quite different from the first.

Stage Three

Drop the counting altogether and simply sit with as full an awareness as you can of the sensation of the whole breathing process.

Stage Four

Focus on the point where you first experience the air as you breathe in. For most people this will be just inside the nostrils (assuming you are breathing in and out through your nose, which is best unless there is some reason, like a heavy cold, that makes this difficult). This is normally quite a subtle sensation, but you should not have much trouble being aware of it once you have deepened your attentiveness with the first three stages. If the third stage is like watching the ocean breaking on the shore, the fourth is like watching a wave break on a rock.

This sensation is, of course, coming and going. And it might be even more subtle going out than going in, because the air is now much the same temperature as the body. So the sensation will wax and wane, but try to keep your attention on the same spot. Unless you become very concentrated you will still be aware of the main body of the breath, so I tend to say to students that it is more a matter of placing an emphasis, or the weight of your attention, on this spot, rather than trying to keep out the broader awareness of the breath.

The regular practice of the Mindfulness of Breathing introduces into our lives an increased sense of spaciousness. We will find that our mind feels less busy. The less busy our mind is, the closer we are to the truth; the more active our mind with chatter, worry, or fantasy, the less aware we are of what is actually going on, both inside us and around us in the world.

The Metta Bhavana

At first, the Metta Bhavana may seem very different from the Mindfulness of Breathing, but the two complement each other very well. Even if we prefer one meditation to the other, which most people do, we will find that practising the one enriches our experience of the other. In the end, they are both about the development of awareness. Let's see if we can get a handle on what is meant by the word *metta*, and then look at the structure of the practice itself.

The Pali word *metta* is often translated 'universal loving-kindness'. Sometimes it is rendered simply as 'friendliness' or, less often, 'love'. I rather like the least common rendering: 'love'. It has drawbacks in that it usually refers to romantic or sexual feelings, which few of us in our culture need consciously to cultivate. But despite these connotations, it has for me a directness and strength that make it seem appropriate.

Bhavana is another Pali word, and means 'cultivation' or 'development'. So this meditation is about the cultivation of *metta*. The idea that we can cultivate some emotions rather than others goes somewhat against the grain in Western society. Most of us think that while we may learn to control the expression of our feelings through discipline or strength of character, we are more or less stuck with the basic way in which we respond to things emotionally. Buddhism does not take this view. The Buddhist view is that while our basic emotional attitudes are quite deep-seated, it is within the reach of all of us to change, if we know how. We just have to make a consistent effort.

So this meditation is concerned with the cultivation of positive emotion. More than that, it is about establishing in ourselves a basically positive attitude towards ourselves and others. While we are often aware that our moods change from day to day, even from hour to hour, we can also probably sense a kind of background emotionality. We all have our ups and downs, but it is clear that different people deal with these fluctuations in very different ways.

The Metta Bhavana is concerned with giving us a positive emotional foundation or background to our lives. To begin with, our practice of this meditation is in great part a kind of investigation of our emotional life. It is the application of increased awareness, mindfulness, and sense of clarity to our emotions. It is not a matter of controlling them, but a slow process of getting to know ourselves, learning to acknowledge who we really are, then encouraging the more expansive and warmer aspects of ourselves.

The Metta Bhavana is a very simple practice. There is nothing difficult about it. It becomes difficult only when we are looking for something that is not there. If we are trying to work with delusion it will be painful. If we want to feel great compassion when in fact we are fed up and depressed, we are creating a gap which will be filled with frustration and pain. If, on the other hand, we start from where we are, we will feel good that the meditation has helped us to shift our negative feelings, even if only a little bit. We will experience a sense of change, a sense that we can work with our feelings. In fact, when we start from a position of honesty, we open up the way for real change to take place, and sometimes we will find that this change can be quite dramatic.

The practice is divided into five stages, and in each stage we direct a feeling of metta towards a different person (or persons, in the case of the final stage).

Stage One

The ability to feel metta towards others is based upon, or is dependent upon, the ability to feel metta towards ourselves. This is therefore where the practice begins. In this stage we cultivate a sense of metta towards ourselves. This might feel quite awkward if we have been brought up to feel that caring for ourselves is selfish.

If you think of someone you know who is selfish, it is unlikely they will strike you as having a deeply loving attitude towards themselves. Selfishness has its roots in a feeling of impoverishment. We feel that everyone else has it better than us, that it's a dog-eat-dog kind of world and we are going to get ours.

Generous people normally seem quite content: they like themselves, they have an inner richness and do not feel depleted by giving to others. Here I am not so much talking about material generosity, which is to some degree dependent on material wealth, and can even be a substitute for real generosity. I am talking about people who make us feel they have time for us, who go out of their way to be helpful. Generosity is a very important part of the Buddhist path, because it is the outward expression of metta. In this sense it is a kind of barometer of mental health. So to cultivate metta towards oneself is the first step towards being less selfish.

In this practice it is important not to think in terms of imposing metta. It isn't a matter of just overlaying our old emotional patterns with a surface film of loving-kindness. The meditation is working towards making deep changes in those patterns, not covering them up, so it has to be done on the basis of how we really feel, not how we would like to feel or how we think we should feel.

So we want to try for an honest, direct experience of how we are at the time we undertake the practice. We want to leave aside ideas about who we are, and concentrate on what we actually experience. Once we feel we're aware of our general state of mind we can begin to think in terms of encouraging metta towards ourselves.

We need to contact a sense of wishing ourselves well, even if we are aware that other feelings are also present, so we begin to work with whatever positive feelings we already have. We are not sitting here like a hanging judge. We have a concern for ourselves as towards a loved friend. We are being tender and open-hearted towards ourselves. It is with this attitude that we work with what we find in our experience. We begin to nurture what is positive, and to give energy to it. We do this by showing an interest in it. No feeling is too small for our interest.

Our happiness has to be based on love towards ourselves, for if it is dependent on the love coming to us from others it will sooner or later break down. We have to learn to like ourselves for what we are, not in comparison with others. When we have positive feelings towards ourselves it becomes much easier to like others; we are not threatened by them, we wish them to be happy as well.

To have sympathy towards ourselves means to be honest – to seek the truth – within a context of understanding and love. We have to be able to recognize our faults and acknowledge that we make mistakes. We don't just shrug them off and get on with making more; we try to see them clearly and at the same time keep them in perspective, recognizing that we are much more than our faults and mistakes, that we also have the capacity to love, to be creative, to give

and to change. If we develop metta towards ourselves we will be able
to see our failings within a broader context and they will not overwhelm us. The same will be true of our attitude towards others.

A common way to develop metta is simply to say a few encouraging words towards oneself: 'May I be well, may I be happy, may I
be free from suffering, may I make progress.' The point of this is, of
course, not just to say the words but to encourage a feeling or emotion
of kindness or warmth towards oneself. This approach works well for
some people, but there are many other methods we can use, which I
discuss in *Change Your Mind*.

Stage Two

Now we bring to mind a good friend, someone whose company we
enjoy. It is said that it is best to choose someone who is about your
own age, still living, and of the same sex. To be on the safe side I
usually suggest you choose someone of your own sex towards whom
you do not have any sexual feelings. These conditions help to keep
this stage of the practice as clear-cut as possible, and most of us will
more easily and naturally feel an affinity with friends of our own sex.
So we bring this person to mind. Don't spend long trying to find
exactly the right person – it is not critical. I normally just say to myself
'a good friend', see who pops up, and go with them – unless it's clear
they don't fit in to this section.

Try to hold this person in mind. Some people find visualization
easy, so this is a good way to keep that person in mind. But if
visualization is a bit of a mystery to you, as it is to me, there are plenty
of other things you can do to evoke this friend. I find I am good at
recalling people's voices, and I often listen, rather than look, for the
friend.

You are trying to hold this friend in your awareness, so if you drift off, this is the point of reference to come back to. Once you feel you have established a degree of contact with your friend, you can wish him or her well. Again you might use words, or you might just feel warmth or love flowing towards them. Of course, you can make a conscious effort to stimulate such feelings, but you can't force them, so don't try to do that. Just be open to what is actually happening. These feelings might be strong or faint; you might feel nothing at all, or even quite inappropriate feelings. The important thing is just to be aware of what is happening.

If you feel you are completely losing your way, take a deep breath, come back to yourself, and start again. This stage will usually be fairly easy; you have chosen someone you care about, so just bearing them in mind should be enough to set going a flow of warmth towards them.

This is a very important stage of the meditation, as it begins to encourage us to spend time with positive feelings, and allow them time and space to grow. How often do we give ourselves this chance to enjoy our feelings of friendliness, to relish our appreciation of someone else? We tend, for some reason, to indulge negative feelings a lot more often. If you think of someone who has recently upset you, you will find, most probably, that you spend a great deal of mental energy on them – a lot more than you do on feelings of friendliness.

Having said that, metta is rather more than just wallowing in our special friendships. Metta is not a 'sticky' thing, so the work in this stage involves letting go of the friend, allowing them to be happy for their own sake, not for ours. We have to try to let go of our expectations of them, our need for them. This is not necessarily all that easy, so we need to be patient with ourselves.

Stage Three

In this stage we bring to mind a different person, this time someone that we could call a neutral person, towards whom we have no strong feelings one way or the other. It might be someone we work with but have never really got to know, or it might be someone we often see in our locality; it doesn't matter. What we are trying to encourage here is an expansion of our normal emotional range, a broadening of our emotional awareness to include those who do not have a direct impact on our lives.

We are trying to experience the same well-wishing towards this person as we do towards our friend. So we are encouraging the beginnings of a basic reorientation of our whole emotional life – a movement away from an emotionality based in a self-referential attitude towards an attitude that is far more open and expansive. I am sure that at some point in our lives we have all experienced metta from a stranger – an act of friendliness free from any selfish motivation. It might be as simple as a smile, or help when we need it.

A word I often use when describing this stage is solidarity. We are encouraging a feeling of solidarity towards others, not because they have a direct effect on our lives, but simply because they too are alive. We know, if we use a little imagination, that these neutral persons share with us the same range of emotions; they have their hopes and fears, their joys and pains, as we do, and it is on the basis of this recognition of our shared humanity that we find the desire to wish them well. I hardly need to point out what a different world we would find ourselves in if we all took the time and trouble (perhaps I should say time and pleasure) to cultivate such feelings towards each other.

Stage Four

We now make a move into enemy territory, that is to say, we bring to mind a person who would normally provoke in us rather unfriendly feelings. We bring to mind an enemy, or at least someone we find difficult or irritating. This is a very interesting stage of the meditation to teach, as it tends to provoke strong reactions in people. These range from denying there is anyone they dislike, to honestly stating that they do not want to wish such a person well, as this would seem hypocritical.

To those who say they don't have anyone they dislike in their life I sometimes suggest they bring to mind a member of their family. This normally gets a laugh of recognition. The problem here is that we tend to think that if we are a 'nice' person we shouldn't have such feelings. But it isn't a matter of what we should or shouldn't have; it is just a fact that these feelings are part of our lot as human beings. It is very unlikely that we don't entertain any negative feelings at all towards anyone. It is much more likely that we do not acknowledge these feelings in ourselves because we think they are bad.

This is important, because it takes a lot of emotional energy to hold down these more negative feelings, and while our energy is being employed to do that, it is not available to us for more useful things. It is relatively easy to transform energy, but that energy must first be available.

I have worked with many deeply depressed people, and very often one of the first signs that the depression is beginning to lift is an upsurge of anger. This is an extreme example, but the principle holds true in more subtle forms. It is as if these feelings are the crudest expression of our emotional energy. The crude ore has to be extracted before the refining process can begin. So don't worry about having these negative feelings – they are the raw material for metta. Nor is there any need to worry if it takes us a little while to free up some of this energy. Once again, don't force it. Trust in the practice.

As for the other extreme – people who frankly admit to strong feelings of hatred or dislike, but do not see why it is in their own interest to work with these feelings – I like to tell them the analogy for hatred in traditional Buddhism. Hatred is likened to picking up a burning log or coal to throw at your enemy: quite possibly you will miss, but you can be sure that you will burn yourself. Hatred is not something we can direct at others without it having a seriously unpleasant effect on ourselves. So even if at first one cannot honestly find an altruistic motive for working with such emotions, there is a good enough reason of self-interest to get us going.

However, this is the stage in which there may be some risk of falsifying what you actually feel. Do not expect great waves of over-whelming love to flow from your heart. It is very nice if they do, but don't imagine they are the norm. It is more likely that you will drift into revenge fantasies; one moment you're sitting there trying to experience loving-kindness, and the next you have an axe in your hands!

If something like that happens, try to see the humorous side of it. Go easy on yourself: just take a breath, centre yourself, and try again. If it's really too much, choose someone else; perhaps you will have to work up to dealing with your *bête noire* gradually. Even when you see the uselessness of hatred it is still difficult to give it up. According to Buddhism, negative attachment is as strong as, if not stronger than, positive attachment. It is often harder to give up what we hate than what we love, so take it easy.

In this stage it's particularly important to stay in touch with what is going on in your body. Usually, negative feelings, as well as positive ones, have a physical component. This is of a great help to us because it gives us another means to work with what is happening. We shall take a closer look at this later, but for now just think about keeping the body relaxed but alert. It's really quite hard to feel anger when you are physically relaxed and open.

Just do your best to wish this person well. You can reflect that there is probably a lot more to this person than the negative aspects on which you pick up. You can also bear in mind that – from a Buddhist point of view at least – trying to wish this person well really means wishing for their happiness, and in particular their spiritual well-being. If that person were happier, more aware, more kind, would you still find them difficult?

Note that in this practice we are wishing people well, not kidding ourselves that really everyone is OK; clearly plenty of people aren't OK. We are simply attempting to break the circle of hatred spawning more hatred.

Stage Five
In the final stage of the meditation we really let ourselves go. We try to apply whatever feelings of metta we have unearthed to all manner of other people, wherever they may be – or, indeed, to all living beings, human and non-human. First of all we bring together the four people we have already included in the meditation, with the thought 'May I feel equal metta for all these people.' This means 'May I feel equally strong metta towards all four people.'

This doesn't mean we stop having particular friends. It doesn't mean we stop enjoying the company of some people more than others. It's just that when we awaken the faculty of metta within us we find that it's impartial. It's not that it's impersonal, but it goes beyond our personal view of things. It is a response deep within us that is activated by any living being. Almost all of us have it anyway to some degree; at our best we respond naturally to the life in others that we find in ourselves.

So in this stage we are developing the element of non-exclusivity in our metta. We imaginatively expand the range of our metta, gradually taking in all beings; wishing all beings well, wishing all beings freedom from suffering, wishing that all beings may make progress towards true happiness.

You can do this geographically, starting perhaps with those sharing the building in which you are meditating, then taking in those living in that street, the locality, the town, the country, the continent, and so on. Or you can do it by first thinking of your friends, then your family, then your acquaintances, and so on. Or you might find another way of expanding outwards. Sometimes this strikes people as rather abstract; we may wonder how we can really extend metta to people we have never met. But if we let go of the limitations we impose on our imagination, we may well find this to be a very powerful experience.

NOTES AND REFERENCES

1 *Samannaphala Sutta*, Digha-Nikaya 2

2 Ryokan, *One Robe, One Bowl: The Zen Poetry of Ryokan*, trans. John Stevens, Weatherhill, New York and Tokyo 1977, p.46

3 See, for example, *Zen Mind, Beginner's Mind*, Weatherhill, New York and Tokyo 1999, pp.90–3

4 Bauby, *The Diving-Bell and the Butterfly*, Fourth Estate, London 1998, pp.95–6

5 'What the heart is like', Miroslav Holub, *Poems Before and After*, trans. Ewald Osers, Bloodaxe Books, Newcastle 1990, p.92

6 Robert A.F. Thurman (trans.), *The Holy Teaching of Vimalakirti, A Mahayana Sutra*, Pennsylvania State University Press, 1976, p.66

7 *Alagaddupama Sutta*, Majjhima-Nikaya 22

8 Paul Reps (compiler), *Zen Flesh, Zen Bones*, Penguin, Harmondsworth 1991, p.17

9 F.L. Woodward (trans), *Udana* i.10

10 *Zen Flesh, Zen Bones*, p.28

11 *Therigatha* 63

12 Paramananda, *Change Your Mind*, Windhorse, Birmingham 1996

FURTHER READING

Meditation

Kamalashila, *Meditation: The Buddhist Way of Tranquillity and Insight*, Windhorse, Birmingham 1996. A comprehensive introduction to Buddhist meditation, very useful as a reference.

Paramananda, *Change Your Mind*, Windhorse, Birmingham 1996. My introduction to meditation and how it can transform our lives.

Nyanaponika Thera, *The Heart of Buddhist Meditation*, Buddhist Publication Society, Kandy 1992. A full and very clear explanation of mindfulness meditation.

Shunryu Suzuki, *Zen Mind, Beginner's Mind*, Weatherhill, New York 1999. My favourite book on meditation. Practical and poetic, it has been a consistent source of inspiration to me for many years.

Buddhism

Lobsang P. Lhalungpa (trans.), *The Life of Milarepa*, Book Faith India, Delhi 1997. An engrossing account of the life of the eleventh-century Tibetan mystic and poet.

Bhikkhu Nanamoli, *The Life of the Buddha*, Buddhist Publication Society, Kandy 1992. One of the best books on the Buddha's life and teachings.

Walpola Rahula, *What the Buddha Taught*, Grove Press, 1994. A very readable introduction to Buddhism with a good selection of traditional texts. A good place to begin an exploration of the Dharma.

Sangharakshita, *The Three Jewels*, Windhorse, Birmingham 1998. An comprehensive introduction to Buddhism, somewhat dense but very rewarding.

Poetry

Elizabeth Bishop, *Complete Poems*, Chatto and Windus, London 1991. One of the great twentieth-century American poets, accessible and humane.

Ryokan, *One Robe, One Bowl: The Zen Poetry of Ryokan*, John Stevens (trans.), Weatherhill, New York and Tokyo 1977. Poetry from the heart; simple, direct, and moving.

Seamus Heaney and Ted Hughes (eds.), *The Rattle Bag*, Faber & Faber, London 1982. My favourite anthology. A wonderful book for those suspicious of poetry.

Miroslav Holub, *The Fly*, Bloodaxe Books, 1987. A good introduction to the work of this Czechoslovakian scientist-cum-poet, sometimes astringent, often insightful.

Related subjects

Italo Calvino, *Italian Folktales*, George Martin (trans.), Penguin, 2000. A delightful book, guaranteed to enrich the imagination.

Antonio Damasio, *The Feeling of What Happens*, Vintage, London 2000. Engrossing if difficult examination of human consciousness from a biological perspective.

James Hillman, *A Blue Fire: Selected Writings*, Perennial (HarperCollins), 1991. Fascinating, provocative, and frustrating, essential reading for the serious soul from one of Jung's foremost contemporaries.

Index

A

activity 7, 9, 17, 86, 104, 150
after-death experience 162
Ajatasattu 10ff
akushala 13
alienation 8f, 17ff, 77, 122
anxiety 90
Apology (Socrates') 9
appreciation 34, 43, 60, 66, 112,
    180
attachment 183
attention 58, *see also* awareness
Auschwitz 121
autumn 98
Avalokita 128
awareness 14, 37, 47, 53, 62, 86,
    105, 108, 138f, 142, 146, 176
    of body 37, 42, 100, 112f
    of breath 168
    of death *see* death
    of others 9, 77, 112, 148
    of self 9, 49, 51, 76, 84
    of walking 115ff
    of world 9, 66
    transformation of 108, 145
    witness 64

B

Bahiya 108
bardo 96f
    fear in 162
    Reality 96
Bardo Thodol 95, 162, 166
Bauby, J.-D. 60
beauty 99, 103, 111
    and body 33ff
bereavement 125ff
big mind 50f, 98, 99
Bimbisara 10
Bishop, E. 135
bliss-bestowing hands 37
bodhicitta 77, 82
Bodhisattva 128
body 153
    awareness of 42, 100f
    and beauty 33ff

body (contd.)
  meditation 36
  sensation 38, 100f
breath 168, 171
Buddha 10, 11, 38, 88, 108
Buddhist teachings 87

C

calm 7
change 89, 95ff, 98, 130
chi 32
communication 149
compassion 99, 127, 128, 140,
  147, 165
competitiveness 56
concentration 171
confidence 9, 56, 57
connectedness 37f, 74, 76
contentment 109ff
corpses 165
cosmetic surgery 35
cosmic mudra 32
creativity 76
Cummings, E.E. 29

D

Dante 157
death 26, 89, 155, 157ff, 165, 169
depression 182
despair 9
detachment 142
Diamond Throne 38
The Diving-Bell and the Butterfly 60
dukkha 124ff

E

Earth Goddess 38
earth-touching mudra 38
ego 97
elements 65
emotion 63, 182
empathy 141
enemy 182
energy 51
enjoyment 52ff, 67
ethics 13
excitement 51
exercises *see* reflection
existential anxiety 158

F

faith 82
fear 18, 89
  of death 157, 160
fish 133ff
freedom 89
funeral 25, 160

G

generosity 177
God 20
going forth 19, 91
grasping 93
greed 19ff, 110

H

habit 143
hands 29ff, 37, 41ff
hatred 183
health 122

heart 79ff
Hercules 150
hermitage 73
Holub, M. 70, 79, 137
honesty 178
hospice 157, 158
humanity 7ff, 59

I

imagination 69ff, 91, 112, 137,
    142, 145, 146
impermanence 89, 130
intensity 72
interconnectedness 152, 166
interdependence 146
interest 50
intimacy 84

J

Jackson, P. 113
Jesus 33
Jivaka 11
Jordan, M. 113
joy 45ff, 109
Jung, C.G. 162

K

karma 13ff
karma vipaka 15f
kindness 42, 62, 112, 130, 141,
    165
Kipling, R. 156
Kisa Gotami *see* bereavement
kushala 13

L

labels 139
Las Vegas 35
letting go 27, 92ff, 113
life 89, 159, 161, 167
listening 149
loach 81f
longing 17
love 99, 175, 178
loving-kindness 112, 140ff, 175ff

M

mantra 53
map 78
Mara 38
materialism 19ff
maturity 166
meaning 72, 76
meditation 7, 47ff, 78, 92, 105,
    113, 119, 123ff, 139, 141, 171ff
    body 36
    enjoyment 52ff
    preparation 61
    walking 106f
mental states 139
metta 140ff, 175ff, *see also* love
Metta Bhavana 175ff
Midas 20
Milarepa 54ff
mindfulness 37, 46, 171, 176,
    see also awareness
Mindfulness of Breathing 171ff
monk and woman story 113
mudra 32, 38
multi-tasking 111

muse 76
mystics 21

N
nature 72, 85, 146
negative emotion 182
Neruda, P. 6, 8
nomads 19

O
openness 19, 50, 79, 95, 127
ox-herding pictures 105

P
pain 39, *see also* suffering
parable 87
Paracelsus 122
pema 140
Plath, S. 156
Plato 9
poetry 136, 142, 145, 156
    beauty 103
    boy's head 70
    Cummings, E.E. 29
    death 155
    greed 19
    hands 29
    heart 79ff
    hermitage 73
    Holub, M. 70, 79, 137
    play 73
    quiet 5
    Ryokan 20, 72ff, 77, 99
    solitude 1
potential 55, 56, 83

R
raft parable 87
reactivity 39
reality 97, 123
rebirth 159, 162
recollection of death 166
reflection 16, 150
    on activity 86, 150
    appreciation 43, 65
    body 100, 152
    breath 168
    change 130
    death 26, 169
    elements 65
    emotion 63
    hands 41ff
    impermanence 130
    interconnectedness 152
    listening 149
    nature
    others 148
    relaxation 67
    ritual 150
    sensation 100
    senses 43
    stillness 23
    time 67
    walking 115ff
    writing 25
reincarnation *see* rebirth
relaxation 67
renunciation 91
ritual 143, 150
Rumi 94
Ryokan 20, 72ff, 77, 99

S

Sacks, O. 31
Sangharakshita 45
security 18
self-awareness 51, 76, 84
self-reflective awareness 49
self-worth 56, *see also* confidence
selfishness 177
sensation 38, 92, 100f
senses 43
sentimentality 140
small mind 98
Socrates 9
solidarity 181
solitude 1
'Song of a Yogi's Joy' 54
'Song of Myself' 16
soul 3, 9, 17, 77, 159, 167
spiritual life 84
spiritual practice 57, 83
stillness 7, 9, 14, 17, 23, 104
story 87
    of Ajatasattu 10
    of Avalokita 128
    of Bahiya 108
    on death 125, 160
    of mustard seed 125
    of raft 87
    of teapot 91
    of two monks and a woman 113
stress 119ff, 123
suffering 124ff
Suzuki, S. 50, 62, 98

T

Tara 128
taste 88
teapot story 91
Thomas, D. 156, 157, 164
Tibetan Buddhism 143
time 67
touch 31, 33
Tozan 107
Tranströmer, T. 2

U

United States 120ff

V

views 93f
Vimalakirti 83
visualization 171
volition 15ff

W

walking 105ff, 115ff
wealth 19
Whitman, W. 16
wisdom 78
witness awareness 64
Wittgenstein, L.J.J. 157
work 121
work ethic 20
writing exercise 25

Z

Zen 32, 37, 105
Zen Mind, Beginner's Mind 62

WINDHORSE PUBLICATIONS

Windhorse Publications is a Buddhist charitable company based in the UK. We place great emphasis on producing books of high quality that are accessible and relevant to those interested in Buddhism at whatever level. We are the main publisher of the works of Sangharakshita, the founder of the Triratna Buddhist Order and Community. Our books draw on the whole range of the Buddhist tradition, including translations of traditional texts, commentaries, books that make links with contemporary culture and ways of life, biographies of Buddhists, and works on meditation.

As a not-for-profit enterprise, we ensure that all surplus income is invested in new books and improved production methods, to better communicate Buddhism in the 21st Century. We welcome donations to help us continue our work – to find out more, go to www.windhorsepublications.com.

The Windhorse is a mythical animal that flies over the earth carrying on its back three precious jewels, bringing these invaluable gifts to all humanity: the Buddha (the 'awakened one') his teaching, and the community of all his followers.

Windhorse Publications	Perseus Distribution	Windhorse Books
169 Mill Road	1094 Flex Drive	PO Box 574
Cambridge CB1 3AN UK	Jackson TN 38301	Newtown NSW 2042
info@windhorsepublications.com	USA	Australia

THE TRIRATNA BUDDHIST COMMUNITY

Windhorse Publications is a part of the Triratna Buddhist Community, which has more than sixty centres on five continents. Through these centres, members of the Triratna Buddhist Order offer classes in meditation and Buddhism, from an introductory to deeper levels of commitment. Bodywork classes such as yoga, Tai chi, and massage are also taught at many Triratna centres. Members of the Triratna community run retreat centres around the world, and the Karuna Trust, a UK fundraising charity that supports social welfare projects in the slums and villages of South Asia.

Many Triratna centres have residential spiritual communities and ethical Right Livelihood businesses associated with them. Arts activities are encouraged too, as is the development of strong bonds of friendship between people who share the same ideals. In this way Triratna is developing a unique approach to Buddhism, not simply as a set of techniques, but as a creatively directed way of life for people living in the modern world.

If you would like more information about Triratna please visit www.thebuddhistcentre.com or write to:

London Buddhist Centre	Aryaloka	Sydney Buddhist Centre
51 Roman Road	14 Heartwood Circle	24 Enmore Road
London E2 0HU	Newmarket NH 03857	Sydney NSW 2042
UK	USA	Australia

Solitude and Loneliness: A Buddhist View
by Sarvananda

Charlie Chaplin observed, 'Loneliness is the theme of everyone.' Although true, it is equally true that we all very skillfully, and often unconsciously, organize our lives in such a way as to avoid loneliness.

Drawing on a wide range of sources – the poets Dickinson and Hafiz, the painter Edward Hopper, the sage Milarepa, the lives of Helen Keller and Chris McCandless, and of course the Buddha – Sarvananda explores the themes of isolation, loneliness and solitude from a Buddhist perspective and examines how and why our relationship to ourselves can be a source of both suffering and liberation.

ISBN 9781 907314 07 0
£8.99 / $13.95 / €10.95
152 pages

Meditating: A Buddhist View
by Jinananda

Meditation is a household word, everyone has their idea of what it is, but does this mean that it is more misunderstood than understood? Here Jinananda, an experienced meditation teacher, gives us the Buddhist perspective. He shows us that – far from being a safe, patching-up, therapeutic tool – meditation is a radical, transformative, waking-up practice.

Buddhist meditation is about being true to your experience, and this means getting behind the idea of what is going on, behind the label, to the ungraspable experience of this moment. Jinananda shows you how to start doing this, how to sit comfortably for meditation, and how to do two meditation practices that develop clarity, peace of mind and positive emotions.

ISBN 9781 9073140 6 3
£8.99 / $13.95 / €10.95
160 pages

Finding the Mind: A Buddhist View
by Robin Cooper

'Here am I, in this body I call my own, among millions that are mysteriously other. What's going on?' You may have asked this, or something like it, at some point in your life. How can you find the answer?

Buddhism points to your own mind as a way to understand and transform your experience. But, as Robin Cooper explains, it takes an exploratory approach, it asks you to seek: it is not a revelation of religious truths. The Buddha saw that we are all in a tough predicament. We are constantly anxious about what we lack and what we may lose, and in chasing security we easily cause pain to others. But the Buddha did not offer to save us through faith in his truth. Instead, he asked us to explore. Be aware, probe the edges of your awareness, investigate, and find your mind.

ISBN 9781 9073140 3 2
£8.99 / $13.95 / € 10.95
160 pages